St. Francis of
856 North
Wichita

THE DOGWALKER

THE
DOGWALKER

by Sophy Burnham

Frederick Warne

New York • London

Frederick Warne & Co., Inc.
New York, New York

Printed in the U.S.A. by Maple Press
Book design by Denise Schiff

Library of Congress Cataloging in Publication Data

Burnham, Sophy.
  The dogwalker.

  SUMMARY: A girl's summer job walking the dog of the Secretary of State involves her in an assassination plot.
  [1. Washington, D. C.—Fiction] I. Title.
PZ7.B9354Do [Fic] 79-13157
ISBN 0-7232-6170-9

Dear Molly,

This book is my present to you. Unfortunately it takes so long to write and publish a book that by the time you hold the printed volume in your hand, you'll probably be too old for the story. But someday when you're grown, you'll be young enough again (because adults are sometimes younger than children).

Then you'll remember how one summer in Georgetown you had a job walking the dog for a Secretary of State and how you won the DC 101 Talent Contest and got a year's free pass to the movies for two. And only you (and Natasha) will know which parts of this book happened and which are made up. And Natasha can't read.

As for geography, if you are clever you will be able to walk the whole map of Cocky's search for Isabel.

The publishing business being what it is, though, I add the sentences all novelists insert: *this story is fictional and any relation to living persons or events is purely coincidental.* And since this holds true for everyone except Harold Sugar at the Dumbarton Pharmacy and Dr. Henry Kissinger, I won't have lied.

S. B.

Chapter 1

Afterward, looking back on it, Cocky couldn't believe that so much had happened in only a few weeks, and it wasn't just her worry over Isabel, or her troubles with her parents, or the fact of falling in love for the first time (though that was nothing like she had imagined it would be, and painful too); no, nor even her meeting with the President of the United States. It was the combination of everything happening at once; and what was most curious was that she was still alive.

It began quietly enough on a quiet street in Washington, D.C., as she paused, one hand on the knob to Dumbarton Pharmacy, wondering if she shouldn't go to People's Drugstore instead. She was dressed as usual in a sloppy T-shirt and a pair of cutoff jeans that frayed into long white strings about her thighs; her dark bangs fell like a shaggy pony's across her eyes, and standing there, feeling the summer heat wash in waves against her skin and ooze into her bones, standing blinking in the dazzling white light, her heart was flooded for a moment with happiness. For that instant she felt as if she had no troubles in the world, except the one that flashed over her at night sometimes, a feeling that time was racing by too fast, was catching up. She did not want to be grown-up. She loved being herself, a girl, a tomboy. If she had her way, nothing in the world would change.

Overhead a plane droned past, interminably slow; and then she opened the door, and the adventure began. She was hit by a blast of air so cold it sucked her breath away and lifted goosebumps on her arms. Harold was on the phone behind the counter. She noted quickly, just in passing, the rich brown bottles that filled the shelves behind him: jars of pills and potions with which he made up his prescriptions. Then she dived for the row of comics at the bottom of the magazine rack.

Cocky had already been up since five that morning, keeping order in her world. First she had met George, the mounted policeman, riding his rangy black horse in the park. George worked for the National Park Service. He rode Leggins in riot control, when there were demonstrations at the Lincoln Memorial or the White House; he paraded in presidential inaugurations and state funerals, directed traffic, and generally impressed the tourists. Once, he had told her, he had "apprehended a mugger" right here in Montrose Park, while riding on his horse. Cocky was impressed.

Now she walked beside him, chatting amiably, one hand stroking the silky fine smooth hair of the big horse's neck, until the path dipped into the woods, and horse and rider cantered off.

That was the first responsibility of her day. The second was to give the sliding board a tryout, sliding on both feet. Then, trotting past the box-bush maze, she veered over to the tennis courts, where a man and woman were vollying, dressed in brand-new whites. They were just beginners. They reached for the ball with elbows out and knees locked stiff. Cocky hung with one hand on the chain-link fence, making faces at them. "You missed," she called out loudly. Or, "Good get." It took almost no time at all for them to decide to leave. Their backs turned to Cocky, they hurriedly pushed their rackets into presses and scurried off. Cocky, whistling, strolled the other way.

By then it was 6:30 A.M. and time to duck down the back alleys and shortcut over a fence to make sure that Mrs. Eustice was shuffling in her bathrobe to the garbage cans to feed stray cats, that Mr. Gault was walking his Airedale slow-ly around the block, that the dew was still dripping from the azalea bushes by the library steps and the rush-hour traffic singing along the highway.

Eventually Cocky had returned to her own two-story brick house, where she had read through three pages of funnies in the *The Washington Post* while slowly chewing a bagel smeared with ricotta cheese and jam. That took some time, but Cocky had plenty of time, for her mother liked to sleep late on Saturdays, especially now with her father gone. Cocky wandered around the house, wishing for the thou-sandth time that the twins down the block had not left for Maine or Liza gone away to summer camp. Practically every-one in the whole world had gone away for the summer.

"Don't you care?" she had asked her mother. "I'm the only person in the whole country practically who's still in Washington."

"Tough," said her mother without a trace of humor. "Go find something to do." And she poured herself her fifth cup of coffee for the day. She had no sympathy for Cocky's plight: a whole summer stretching ahead of her, and no one around to play with.

Cocky offered the cat some jam, scratched its ears in boredom, and then, remembering that her mother liked to know her plans, she scribbled a quick note: "Gone out," it said, as if the back door left standing open did not attest the fact.

So now Cocky was sitting cross-legged on the floor of Dumbarton Pharmacy, absorbed in comic books. In her pocket was fifty cents from her allowance, and facing her was the choice of which one she should buy.

Most did not interest her. She liked Archie comics and Uncle Scrooge. She hated monster comics, science fiction, and all superheroes except Wonder Woman. She had retarded tastes. That's what Liza, her best friend at school, told her. She picked out three comics and began to read.

Sometimes Cocky would read all the comics she wanted and then spend her money on bubble gum instead. Sometimes she glanced through the big magazines, like *Mademoiselle* or *Seventeen*. They seemed pretty childish to her. They concentrated mostly, she decided, on how to have a glowing complexion, how to get a boy, or how to behave on a date. The women's magazines, like *Redbook* or *McCall's*, were just as bad, except they told how to keep a glowing complexion, how to get a husband, and behave as a wife. Only they never wrote about the high forced brittle laughter, or the hours locked in the bathroom crying. Cocky could hear her mother's sobs even with the door closed, and she would cover her ears with her pillow as she lay in bed at night.

Cocky wondered if adults ever grew up. She had spent a lot of time thinking over the matter, and it seemed to her that there must be more to life than knowing how to behave with a boy. Like adventure. When she grew up, she would have adventures. She was going to do something so exciting that her name would be on everyone's lips. She would be on the cover of *Time*, and the television news reporters would come to her house to interview her. It would take place at night; the TV cables would snake like firehoses up and down the block, and there she would be, standing at her front door, squinting in the blinding white lights at the blurred, pale faces below. "It was really nothing," she would say, while the crowd erupted into wild applause.

Cocky couldn't imagine what she would do. But one thing for sure: knowing how to put on mascara would be low on the list of necessary skills. In fact, Cocky had an idea that wearing mascara would get in the way of her adventures. Mascara runs. She knew that because she had once seen an article on how to swim at the beach with "your guy" without having your mascara run. She had read the article all the way through, and sure enough, the one guaranteed way to keep mascara from running was never mentioned: don't wear any.

"Cocky?" She jumped at Harold's voice. "You were looking for a job, weren't you?"

"Yes. I still am." She stood up.

"Well, Mrs. Stinson was in here awhile ago. She's looking for someone to walk her dog. You want to do it?"

"Sure." Cocky had never thought of dogwalking. "What do I do?"

"Just go apply and see if you get the job," he answered. "It's Mrs. Stinson, down on Dumbarton Street. Tell her I sent you."

"Do you have the phone number?"

"It's unlisted. But I think I have an address." He spun his wheeldex of customers, jotted down an address, and handed it over the counter to Cocky. "She's a nice dog. You'll like her."

"Oh, thanks. And can I have this comic?" She pulled two quarters from her pocket.

"Cocky Norton," he laughed, "aren't you ashamed of reading comics at your age?"

But Cocky just grinned, turned to the door, then paused. "Who is Mrs. Stinson?" she asked. "That name is so familiar."

"I don't know who *she* is," Harold said. "But her husband is the Secretary of State." At which Cocky felt her stomach drop.

Chapter 2

Cocky closed the pharmacy door behind her. The Secretary of State is the second most important official in Washington, if you count the President as first. She wasn't sure she wanted the job. Cocky knew about Secretaries of State.

No one can live in Georgetown and not be aware of the power of the government. It surrounds you. Limousines pull up to the curb, disgorging women dressed in silk print dresses and wearing fixed bright smiles and behind them their husbands, important officials with lined, anxious faces and distracted looks. That was what Cocky noticed most about them: that blind impersonal stare, as if they could not see.

Then too there are the constant bodyguards.

A new Secretary of State is appointed by each President. Cocky remembered when Dr. Henry Kissinger was Secretary of State and lived right around the corner from her in a house on P Street. She was only a little girl then, but she knew a lot of people were impressed with his moving in. Mrs. Pearson, who was shaped like a lovely Easter egg—and dressed like one too, in wild splashy patterns—had walked her terrier past the Kissinger house ten times a day: the dog had never had so much exercise.

Before Dr. Kissinger moved in, the Secret Service had inspected the entire neighborhood. An agent had come to the

Nortons' door, neat as a Bible salesman in his gray suit and white tie. In one hand he held an open wallet with his I.D. card.

"Secret Service," he snapped efficiently.

"Secret Service!" The very idea broke Cocky up. She pushed through the open door onto the front steps. "Can I see?"

"Cocky!" Her mother's voice rose warningly. "Behave." Then to the stranger: "May I help you?" she asked coolly, smoothing back a lock of her hair which was brown then and shoulder-length.

"Yes, ma'am." The Secret Service prides itself on courtesy. The agent dropped his wallet into a back pocket. "You probably know that the Secretary of State has bought a house around the corner—"

"Which house?" Cocky interrupted. "I haven't seen a house for sale."

The agent looked down at her in surprise. "It's on P Street," he said with a vague wave of his hand. "This is just a routine check." He turned back to Mrs. Norton. "We want you to know that we'll be around, that he will have twenty-four-hour, round-the-clock protection, and all we want is to ask for your help."

"Yes, of course," Mrs. Norton murmured uncertainly.

"If you see anyone suspicious hanging around the neighborhood, any strangers, anyone you haven't seen before—"

"Any strangers!" Cocky burst out laughing. "The Secretary of State moves one block from the busiest shopping street in Washington, and you want us to watch out for strangers!" She flung herself helplessly down the steps to the street and doubled over laughing.

"Katharine," her mother said. It was one firm word, but Cocky drew up short.

The security agent let his eyes drift absently down the street, as if in pain. Then he recollected himself. "Well, if you see anyone suspicious, will you please telephone this number?" He thrust out a small white card. "Thank you." He stepped back into the street.

The encounter was clearly at an end, and Cocky leaped up the steps and squirmed over beside her mother to read what was on the card. "What does it say?" she asked, as the door closed behind her.

"It says, if you see any strangers, or anyone acting in an unusual fashion, to call 911."

"Call 911! That's the police!" Cocky could barely contain her laughter. "I'm going to do it," she shouted. "I'm going to go find a stranger right this minute and call the police."

"Katharine Anne Norton! You come right back here this instant!" But it was no use. Her daughter, in a flash of bare feet and jeans, had disappeared out the door and around the corner.

After that, Cocky made a point of teasing the Secret Service agents stationed outside Kissinger's house.

At Halloween she soaped the camera eye above the Kissinger door. During the year she trailed the bodyguards whenever she came across them with the Secretary of State.

The agents wore little radios in the left breast pockets of their jackets, with a wire running up to one ear, and they walked briskly behind Dr. Kissinger, their chins twisted onto their left shoulders and talking in undertones to their pocket handkerchiefs.

Cocky stumbled two steps behind them. "One . . . two . . . there are three . . . no, four agents behind the Secretary of State," she reported loudly to her own left shoulder. "And two more across the street sitting in a black Lincoln limousine." Once she counted ten agents in all, some carrying briefcases as a disguise.

One winter day Cocky was skating along the sidewalk ice in sneakers, when she came to the guard at the Kissinger house. He stood erect and purposeful, cupping his cigarette in the palm of his hand.

"You ought to clear the sidewalk," she told him, skidding to a stop. "Don't you know it's against the law to leave snow and ice on the sidewalk in front of your house?"

The agent stared over her head into the middle distance.

"Besides," Cocky continued happily, "you could personally get into a lot of trouble. For instance, I could slip and fall right now and break my back, and you'd have to bring me inside the house for emergency treatment, and then I'd have a bomb under my coat and blow everybody up. It's dangerous, having ice outside your house. You could lose your job."

"*Hmph.*" For an instant, his eyes glanced across at her, his moustache quivering with distaste. Then he settled more firmly onto both feet and stared at the roofs across the street. Cocky skated on, but later that evening on her way home, her heart leaped up—it skipped a beat on seeing the agent standing in the snowy dusk, flinging salt with wide swings of his arm up and down the Kissinger walk.

Cocky was never serious. She did not know that the agents knew her name, address, and age; or that when the men were off-duty and lounging in the shabby second-hand furniture in the Kissinger basement that served as their duty room, they talked of her in language unfit for children's ears.

"You won't guess what that Norton kid did today."

"I don't want to know."

"She told me I couldn't park the car in the Secretary's no-parking zone because it was reserved."

"You know them maple seed pods—what we used to call 'flags' when we was kids?" said one agent. "Well, today she stuck one on the top of her nose, and she has two more dragging down from each nostril and she comes over to me, leering, and her eyes crossed like a looney, and making all these *goo-goo ga-ga* sounds at me."

They told each other grimly what they'd like to do to her if they weren't in government service.

It was only later that Cocky learned that the agents carried machine guns in those briefcases, or that a man had been killed once while reaching for his pipe, when an agent suspected a terrorist attack. By then Kissinger had moved to New York, followed by his guards, and Cocky had grown older too. The Secret Service no longer patrolled her block, and since the President had changed, so too had the Secretary of State.

Cocky stared at the slip of paper in her hand: the address of John Baron Stinson, Secretary of State. It was one thing to tease his Secret Service as a child. It was quite another to assume responsibility for his dog.

Chapter 3

Cocky approached the Stinson block moving cautiously, light as a cat. She was casing the joint. The houses stood on a hill above the street, each reached by a long flight of steps. They were huge. They extended back from the street almost one full block, and behind the houses were large gardens and garages.

Cocky had watched detectives on TV. She knew how the most innocent person could be wiped out if he weren't careful—one false step and the machine guns of either police or mob would sweep the streets, leaving a path of blood and gore. The gutters would run red with blood.

Now she knelt suddenly and pretended to tie her shoelace. She had spotted the Stinson house. It was a big gray Victorian structure, jutting with a dozen odd angles, battlements, dormer windows poking out from the roofs, and, to her delight, a round tower on one corner. An alley ran along the side of the house.

Cocky crossed the street, heading toward the house. Casually she pulled a rubber ball from her shorts pocket and began to bounce it at her feet. She wished Liza were with her. Down the block a woman was struggling to pull a bag of groceries out of the back seat of her Volkswagen, and somewhere in the distance a dog barked. When it stopped, the street seemed to ring with silence.

"One, two, button your shoe . . ." Cocky sang the first thing that came to mind. She glanced about, trying to spot the security guards. None were in sight.

"Five, six, pick up sticks. *Oooh!*" The ball flew awkwardly out of her hands and rolled down the slight incline into the alley beside the Stinson house.

"Oh dear, my ball!" Cocky spoke very loudly to a clear summer sky. She skipped after the ball into the alley and with a quick, neat kick drove it to the far end.

Following slowly, Cocky saw that it was not so much an alley as a driveway, large enough for a single car to pass. It took a sharp right-hand turn behind the garden and came to a dead end at a gate marked by three green plastic garbage cans. Cocky could see no closed-circuit TV cameras either.

She leaped up, grabbed the top of the Stinson fence, and chinned herself until she could see over the top. Below her was a large L-shaped garden. It held a cherry tree, forsythia and azaleas, roses, box and yew, geraniums in flowerpots, and hanging baskets of petunias. But Cocky knew none of the flowers by name, and anyway, they held no interest for her. What struck her was the tent. It was made of canvas, striped yellow and white, and it was perfectly round with a high peaked roof, like the shelter of a Saracen chief, or the pavilion of a medieval king. She sucked in her breath in awe. What a private, secret place.

She fell back to the ground, scooped up her ball, and strolled thoughtfully out of the alley. As she approached the front door of the big house, she spotted the first TV camera, hidden in the shrubbery. Halfway up the steps was another. She passed them both without a glance and had just lifted her hand to ring the doorbell when she was startled by a voice.

"Who is it?"

She jumped. The intercom was just above her ear. She stood on tiptoe to answer.

"I'm Cocky Norton," she said nervously. "I live around

here, and I've heard that Mrs. Stinson is looking for someone to walk her dog."

There was silence. After a moment the intercom crackled again. "Just a minute."

Cocky stared at the stone doorstep, at the windows on either side of her, which were closed off by venetian blinds and then by heavy draperies. Above her head still another closed-circuit camera studied her actions. She shifted uneasily. Then the scrape of a lock, the rattle of chains—and she felt suddenly very small.

The door opened a crack. A dark face peered out at her suspiciously, then the door closed again as the chain lock was removed. When it swung wide, Cocky saw a maid in blue uniform, large, impassive. She did not smile.

Hesitantly Cocky held out the paper Harold had given her. "Is Mrs. Stinson in?"

"Do you have an appointment?"

Cocky lifted one hand to brush her unmanageable hair out of her eyes: a furious swipe. It did no good. Her shaggy mane fell back instantly.

"No," she was saying earnestly. "I heard from Harold at the drugstore that she was looking for someone to walk her dog. I thought . . ." Her voice trailed off. She was filled with hopelessness. Whatever had possessed her to come here?

"Just a minute."

The door closed. Again Cocky was alone. She turned to survey the street. Standing high above the sidewalk like this, she could see into the front gardens of the houses across the street and, except for one tree, her view up and down the block was uninterrupted. She felt as if she were standing at the edge of a cliff. She had just decided to quit, to run down the steps and away, when the door behind her opened again.

"Hello?" It was an older woman, her white hair perfectly in place. She wore a thin summer dress and high heels. On one hand flashed a diamond ring and two emeralds, on her wrist a gold watch, and around her neck a double strand of pearls. "I'm Mrs. Stinson," she said sweetly.

Cocky burst into a wide smile of relief. "I'm Cocky Norton. I heard—"

"I know," said Mrs. Stinson. "Won't you come in?"

And Cocky set foot in the house of the second most important man in Washington.

Later Cocky was teased outrageously for noticing nothing about the house.

"Well, what did it *look* like?" her mother had asked, and turning to her best friend, Mrs. Barr, she'd laughed till Cocky squirmed with annoyance. "Can you imagine?" her mother shrieked. "There she is in the house of the Secretary of State, and she can't remember *any*thing."

"It looked like any old house," she answered. "It had a blue rug."

"A blue rug!" screamed Mrs. Barr, throwing herself back on the couch and spreading her thighs in the way that Cocky hated. "Now I know it's hard"—Mrs. Barr leaned forward on the couch toward Cocky, pressing her fingertips patiently together—"but try to remember!" Then she burst out laughing. "Can you imagine how many people would pay ten or twenty dollars for a view of that house?"

Cocky shrugged. Those were grown-ups, and if they wanted to put down good money to gawk at the Oriental rugs and point out to each other the three-panel black lacquer Chinese screen in the living room or the hunt board in the dining room, that was another indication of their general childishness. Cocky had better things to look at than those.

But she did remember the rug. First, because the soles of her sneakers stuck to it as she entered the house, so that she pitched forward, caught her hip with a sharp quick stab against a table, and sent a lamp crashing to the floor. Second, because while Mrs. Stinson was picking up the lamp, Cocky had a chance to see the dog, seated on the same blue wall-to-wall carpeting at the head of the stairs.

The dog was black, white, and brick-red. Its legs were incredibly short, its ears so long they touched the floor. And the eyes—the eyes, drooping, mournful, liquid brown—were rimmed with red.

"Here, Isabel." Mrs. Stinson had patted her plump hands together and leaned forward as if speaking to a baby. "Come on down."

The sound that rose from the dog's full chest was so extraordinary it raised the hair on Cocky's head. It was not a bark so much as a howl, a single wail that hit her ears and sank like a stone to her chest. The howl of a basset hound. At the same time the chunky dog lifted its hindquarters three inches off the floor (thus standing up) and lunged down the steep staircase toward her. It didn't walk down the stairs. It *rippled*, its stumpy legs moving so fast that Cocky could hardly see them, and its heavy body weaving back and forth so that the front end seemed to be going in a different direction from the rear.

"Isn't she ridiculous?" Mrs. Stinson beamed fondly, but Cocky had already thrown herself forward to meet the dog, and the two tangled into a knot of hands, ears, tail, tongue, and squirming bodies.

"Oh, she's beautiful."

"Her name is Isabel."

"Isabel." Cocky laughed as a long pink tongue rolled across her mouth, a hard whip of a tail lashed her eyes. "Hey, hey." She rubbed both hands down the dog's hard muscular back and caught the thin quick tail.

"She gets no exercise at all," Mrs. Stinson was saying. "She's much too fat. Well, you can see. She just lies down whenever she can."

It was true. Exhausted by her effort, Isabel had collapsed onto the powder-blue carpet and rolled wearily onto her back, her stubby paws in the air. Cocky rubbed her stomach happily, while the dog looked first at her mistress, then at Cocky, her bloodshot eyes half closed in exquisite delight.

"I guess she's fat," answered Cocky, rising to her feet. "I've never seen a dog like this."

"She's a basset, and they *are* heavy. They always have wrinkles. Look." Mrs. Stinson reached down to pick up a handful of Isabel's skin. "They have the *loosest* skin. But she is just a wee bit too fat, I'm sorry to say." She sighed. "We have to travel a lot, the Secretary and I, that's the trouble." She patted Isabel while Cocky mulled over the curious formality of calling your husband by his title instead of his name. She wondered if it was required for all government officials. For instance if the wife of the President had to start saying "Mr. President" after he was elected instead of David or darling or whatever she had called him before. Somehow it was even worse to call your husband "the Secretary," as if he were a typist or something.

She jerked her thoughts back to the present.

"The Secretary is terribly busy now," Mrs. Stinson was saying. "And there's no one here to walk Isabel. Except Charlotte." She gestured toward the kitchen. "Charlotte opened the door for you. I don't know what we'd do without her. She's been with us for years. But I can't ask her to walk the dog. And now we have all these lunches and dinners to give. Or go to." She heaved a helpless sigh and twisted the enormous emerald on her finger. "Really, I don't think I'd have let my husband take this job if I'd known how much work was involved." Her laugh was a little tinkle. Cocky thought she was charming.

"Can't the Secret Service walk her?"

"Oh, no. No." Mrs. Stinson was shocked. "Oh, no, that wouldn't be right at all." She dropped to her heels to run one perfectly manicured hand over Isabel's head. "Oh, no. Of course they accompany us if we go out for a walk, but no, we couldn't ask them to walk the dog. No. No."

"Oh."

"Well, now." Mrs. Stinson rose in a businesslike way, folding one bejewelled hand over the other. "What I want is to have some nice girl—or some nice boy for that matter"—she gave her tinkling laugh—"give Isabel a walk every morning and every evening. It won't be easy. She hates to walk. But we've got to take some fat off her or she'll have a heart attack."

Cocky nodded. "Okay."

"Oh. Can you do that?" Mrs. Stinson sounded surprised.

"Sure."

"Well, then, that's settled." She sounded relieved. "Good. I'll pay you a dollar fifty an hour, and if things work out, I'll give you a raise later. Is that enough? Do you think that's fair?"

"That's fine!" Was it enough? Cocky could have laughed out loud. She would have paid for the chance to walk Isabel. "She's so beautiful—"

"Very well. Then an hour each morning around nine and another at four or five in the afternoon. You can begin today, if you like."

"I'll begin right now, if it's okay."

"Well, fine!" Mrs. Stinson nearly squirmed with pleasure. In a way she reminded Cocky of the dog. "I'll just get you her leash. You know, dear"—she reached out and pushed Cocky's hair off her forehead—"if you got your hair out of your eyes you'd be a very pretty girl."

But Cocky pulled away in irritation. She concentrated on patting Isabel.

Chapter 4

When Mrs. Stinson said it would be hard to walk Isabel, she wasn't telling the half of it. At every curb the little sod sank slowly to the earth like a dying balloon. If they walked as far as a block, Isabel rolled over on one side to relieve her paws of her massive weight.

"Get up, Isabel! Up!"

The dog looked at Cocky with sorrowful brown eyes. Her forehead sagged into a maze of folds and wrinkles, and her large black nose settled sadly on her paws.

Cocky's heart melted. "Oh, Isabel." She dropped to the sidewalk beside the dog. "Do your feet hurt? I'll dust them with talcum when we get home." She bent over until her dark hair fell across Isabel, leaving the dog awash in wonderful smells: breakfast bacon, sugar cookies, Ritz crackers, mud, a gray male cat, and sour sweaty sneakers worn without socks. "Dear Isabel," murmured Cocky, closing those rheumy eyes with one gentle hand. "Don't look so sad."

Isabel inhaled Cocky's own indescribable scent and sank into blissful reverie; for what did it matter if her eyes were closed? She relied for information on her nose. All the news that came to Isabel—the aroma of garbage rotting in the sun, the beer and baloney, the dog droppings in the gutter, and oil and burned rubber on the streets—was reported to her through her large black nose; and to Isabel all these high, fine odors wafting in the summer air smelled marvelous. They rose

18

around her now, more than making up for the fact that even when Cocky's hair was not covering her face she could hardly see. Those sad brown eyes were weak. To the hefty dog the world moved past in a blurry haze. Colors and shapes swam up before her eyes and off again. She leaned her weight against Cocky, breathing in that distinctive smell, her gentle smile. Isabel blinked and the face floated out of focus . . .

"Come on, Isabel! Get *up!*" Isabel rose and followed the blue braided leash that ran from her collar to Cocky's hand up ahead.

At the end of one week Isabel could walk around the block without complaining. At the end of three she could walk for almost an hour without a rest. She loved the walks! Each morning she lay with her nose pressed to the front door, waiting for Cocky. Each afternoon she woke from her nap at five minutes before four and stumbled down the stairs to the door. How she knew the time no one knows; but there she was each day, and when she heard Cocky's step outside, she broke into furious barking that brought from Cocky on the other side of the door a similar tirade. "Isabel! *Wow!* Isabel! *Wow-wow!*" she'd call through the door, until Charlotte undid the bolts and locks and let the two creatures loose on God's green earth.

By then they had already met the boy. It happened like this. Isabel was trotting along on her leash. Her tail whipped in a happy circle above her back. Her nose wound up and down the sidewalk, reading the signs of the animal world; a German shepherd . . . two cats . . . and *salami!*

Isabel stopped dead. It was just in reach. She stepped off the curb into the street. There came a rumble of wheels and Cocky's scream, another deeper yell, a form flying past her head; she ducked, howled, was flattened to the street, a searing pain ripping at her ribs. Then there was silence, except for the dull whir of spinning metal wheels.

"What you think you're doing?" It was a boy's angry voice. Isabel peered into the foggy distance. Cocky lay on the street and beside her sprawled a boy. He smelled of leather, hot metal ball-bearings, grease, plastic, cotton, and a crushed chocolate bar.

"What am *I* doing?" Cocky screamed, but he drowned her out.

"Do you always stop in the middle of the street?"

"Listen, you twerp—"

"No one ever teach you to look?"

"If you can't handle a skateboard—"

"Just don't cross my path." He rose, snatching up his skateboard. He wore a blue and white helmet, Cocky noticed, and his knees and elbows were protected with heavy professional pads. On his hands, despite the summer heat, he wore thick leather gloves.

"Listen, buddy." Her chin jutted aggressively. "Don't you tell me—"

"Don't you buddy me—"

They were squared off now for the fight.

"Oh, yeah? Says who?"

"Says me."

Isabel strained forward toward the scrap of meat. Her tongue extended, curled around the salami like an elephant's trunk—and it was gone. She licked her chops. Delicious. Above her head the two humans circled each other dangerously.

"You dork," sneered Cocky. "Don't cross *me!*"

"Cross you? You can't cross the street!" The boy was taller than Cocky, and his blue eyes flashed with anger.

Cocky drew one sneakered toe along the macadam. "Cross that line—" She made a fist. "You'll get the Folded Five!" She danced from foot to foot, at the ready. "Go on, I dare you. I dare you—" But just then she heard the car bearing down on her, horn blaring. She leaped aside, nerves tingling in the squeal of tires, the high-pitched Doppler shriek that rose, enveloped her, and dropped an octave as the car swerved past.

"Isabel!" For an instant the dog was lost under the wheels of the car; then she was revealed, flat on her side in the street.

"Isabel!" Cocky screamed again. The dog lifted her head and proceeded to lick her ribs, where the skateboard had hit. Cocky's knees went weak with relief. She bent over Isabel and buried her face in the warm neck. A moment later she was aware that the boy was watching her, scowling. She lifted her nose. "Hmph," she said. "Come on, Isabel. Riff-raff."

He stood looking after her. Then suddenly from his throat tore an Indian yell: *"Heeeeeaaaaaaaaa!"* The next moment he had passed her like the wind, swaying down the street on his skateboard. His arms were wide, his knees bent low, and he swooped down the hill picking up speed. Cocky held her breath watching him. He was really good.

Afterward, trudging home with Isabel, she was filled with discontent. Already she could think of a dozen things she wished she'd said. Better, more biting words.

She wondered who he was and why she had never seen him before. Certainly he didn't attend her school. She spat on her scraped elbow, picking at the dirt embedded in the bloody skin, and then, throwing herself to the pavement, she gave Isabel a big bear hug. "Oh, Isabel, I'm so glad you're all right," she murmured.

She wondered if she would ever see the boy again. She wished she'd smashed his face in.

Her mother said Cocky was a "slow bloomer, thank heavens," for certainly she had plenty of friends who liked boys, who talked about them at lunch and flirted with them at school, and some who even went to the movies with boys that they were "going with." Cocky scorned the opposite sex.

Take, for example, Charles, who waited at the bus stop with her for the schoolbus. Charles was a year older than Cocky, and on seeing her he erupted into dizzying gymnastics. He leaped in the air and clapped his heels together, or he dropped to the ground in an awkward crabwalk and snatched at her ankles. Or he tickled his armpits and loosed a series of hair-raising monkey shrieks.

"Stop it, Charles." Cocky thought he was a pain. When the bus came he would vault inside, flop on his back in the last seat, and not speak until his friend B.J. got on ten minutes later.

But what was odd was what happened when he didn't know Cocky was around. A couple of times she had come up on him unawares. Then his body sagged into a cave-man slouch. He seemed so tired he had to lean on the nearest wall or the shoulders of a friend. Charles hardly ever stood on both his feet at once.

Cocky thought Charles was dumb. On the other hand she'd been sort of sorry when he moved away at the end of the school year. She'd named the black horse in one of her posters "Charles" and moved it to the foot of the bed.

Her feelings about the new boy, however, were entirely different. He made *her* feel dumb.

Chapter 5

Two days later Cocky saw the Secretary of State. She was pretending to be a horse, prancing slightly, on her way to Isabel's. At the corner she shied at a leaf, pricked her ears as a spirited pony might do, then stepped delicately forward, one cautious hoof at a time, blowing through her lips: *Prrrrrr-prrrrrrrrr*—this being an easier pony sound to make than a full-fledged neigh.

When she looked up, the Secret Service agent was watching her with a puzzled frown. She was mortified. She turned away, and to her relief saw the agent likewise turn and stroll back down the block toward the Stinsons' house.

It was then that Cocky saw the Secretary of State. He was hurrying down the steps of his house to a waiting limousine.

Cocky dawdled as if absorbed in reverie. She was as abstracted as light and air. In actual fact her entire attention was riveted on the Secretary of State. She recognized him from his pictures in the paper: a tall, distinguished, graying gentleman, dressed in gray suit and vest. He was hurrying down the steps talking to a younger man beside him. On the sidewalk they paused to count the suitcases lined up beside the car. The young man held up one hand, said something, and raced back up the steps two at a time. Mr. Stinson proceeded to the car.

By now Cocky had approached close enough to observe

how his shoulders sagged forward, as if under a weight. He nodded to his chauffeur, who held the back door open. Gracefully he sank into the back seat and disappeared from Cocky's view.

She was intrigued. Clearly the Secretary was going on a trip. She counted five leather suitcases and two briefcases on the brick sidewalk. A single Secret Service agent strolled up and down a short distance away; the chauffeur stood at the open door.

"Buck." Mr. Stinson stuck his head out of the car, addressing the Secret Service agent. "Will you go hurry up Andrews?"

The agent sprinted up the steps.

At that moment the short, stocky man came hurrying toward them. He passed Cocky so quickly his briefcase banged against her leg, making her yelp softly with pain. But he never paused. He glanced at his watch, and suddenly he was tripping on the Stinson sidewalk, falling in a jumble of suitcases. The whole thing was over in a moment—his quick recovery, his mumbled apology as he righted the numerous brown leather bags: "How stupid of me." He smiled apologetically at the chauffeur, who had leaped forward to help him up. He brushed off his knees, gave one quick, curious glance at the Secretary of State seated inside the limousine, and was scurrying down the street again. Up at the Stinsons' front door the Secret Service agent had turned, hand automatically reaching for his jacket pocket. Now he relaxed. The man was halfway down the block by then, once again glancing at his watch, fretting over the time.

It was over, the entire episode, in just an instant—except for Cocky, whose heart had skipped a beat. Was it possible? But she was certain: the briefcase in that man's hand belonged to the Secretary of State, while the matching scuffed leather case on the sidewalk was the one he had originally been carrying in his hand!

Cocky could hardly breathe. Had she really seen it right?

No one seemed to notice! The Secret Service agent dashed down the steps to stroll nonchalantly up and down, the chauffeur turned to look toward the house, and now here came the young man, Andrews, out the Stinson door—

"Wait!" The word stuck in her throat. She was riveted to the spot.

From the corner of her eye, Cocky caught a swinging movement, the glimpse of a body swaying toward her. It passed, then swerved back with a graceful turn. It was the boy.

"Hey, you." His skateboard hit the curb, and he stepped off lightly beside her. "Hey—"

But Cocky was trembling with excitement. "Look." She grabbed his wrist. "Quick."

He could not have been more surprised, but something in Cocky's voice held him, and Cocky herself was so shaken, so absorbed by what she had seen, that she seemed not to recognize him.

"Quick," she ordered. "Pretend we're talking, but watch those men over there."

The boy was sharp. He leaned one hand casually on the wall behind Cocky and half-turned toward her. From that position he could see the whole street. Cocky took the skateboard out of his hand and began to turn it carefully, as if discussing wheels.

"That's the Secretary of State." Her voice was tight. "The man in the limousine. He's going on a trip, and his assistant just ran back in the house for something. That's him coming down the steps. The other man's Secret Service."

"Where's he going?"

"I don't know. But I was just walking along and something happened. A man came by and took one of his brief-cases."

Andrews and the chauffeur were packing the bags in the trunk of the car.

"You're crazy!" St. Francis of Assisi School
856 North Socora
Wichita , Kansas   25

"They haven't even noticed!" Cocky burst out.

"A man took one of their briefcases?"

Cocky looked at the boy, nodding. Again she was startled by his blue-gray eyes framed by black lashes. She noticed he had black hair too.

"Let's walk closer," she said miserably. "This is a nice skateboard."

"The best."

Andrews threw the last of the bags in the trunk, slammed the door, then stuck his head in the back door where the Secretary sat. "All set." His words floated clearly to Cocky and the boy. He nodded to the chauffeur, climbed in the car, and shut the door. The Secret Service agent scowled at the two young people, swept the street once with a searching look, then leaped into the front seat. The car pulled from the curb, proceeded with slow dignity down the street, turned the corner, and disappeared.

Cocky chewed one ragged fingernail nervously. "Oh Lord, what do I do now?" She looked helplessly at the boy.

"Tell me what happened again. I don't understand."

"I don't know," she cried in agitation. "I was just walking down the street real slow, watching everyone get packed up to leave, and the younger man had forgotten something, so he ran back up the steps and inside the house, and the Secretary of State got in his car and the other two men were just hanging around, waiting, when all of a sudden this man came zooming past me. He knocked into me and smashed my leg with his briefcase, and he was just tearing down the street and then just as he reached the car he tripped and fell down all in a heap in the middle of the suitcases, and when he stood up again he was carrying the wrong one."

"He what?"

"Yes," she said. "Yes! He'd exchanged it for one of the ones on the sidewalk. He pretended to trip, and while the chauffeur was helping him up, he sub—he subst—"

"Substituted?"

"Yes, he substituted his briefcase for one of theirs. He left his on the sidewalk and he took one just like it that belonged to the Secretary of State."

The boy looked at her in disbelief. "Are you making this up?"

She was close to tears. "No. I saw it."

He was silent for a moment, watching her. "They must know what they're doing."

"I don't know," she said.

"Or else if the suitcases really matched," he continued, "you made a mistake and *thought* you saw a switch."

She searched her memory for a clue, but the more she tried to remember what had happened the less she trusted what she'd seen. Had he switched the bags? Perhaps she had not even seen the man fall down! Perhaps there had been no man—*No!* She pulled herself up short. Of course there was a man, because her leg still hurt where his case had hit. And yet she was so uncertain of her memory she didn't know anymore what had happened. How absurd to think that he had switched the bags! Things like that don't happen in real life.

"I must have been mistaken," she mumbled. "I must have seen it wrong." She spun the skateboard wheels idly with one hand. "Oh, here." She thrust the skateboard toward him. "I forgot I was holding it."

"That's okay." They were walking toward the Stinson house side by side. "What's your name?" he asked.

"Cocky Norton. I live up on Thirty-first." He nodded and said nothing. Then they were both struck with embarrassment. Cocky flushed and, giving a queer little laugh that sounded as foolish to her own ears as she imagined it did to his, "Well, I gotta go." She glanced up the steps. "I have to walk a dog."

"Oh."

"I walk the dog for the Secretary of State. That's why I was coming over here."

"Is that the dog I tripped over the other day?"

"Yes." Cocky laughed. "That's Isabel. If you wait, you can have a second chance." The next minute she was racing up the steps to the Stinsons' front door. Her heart was pounding, but whether it was caused by the dash up the steps or by the boldness of her invitation to the boy she did not care to know.

"Who is it?" said the intercom.

"It's me. Cocky," she called. From the other side of the door she could hear Isabel bouncing, voice lifted in joyous howls. "*Wow* Isabel," she called. "*Wow-wow.*" As she waited for the door to open, she looked down the steps to the street below. The boy with exquisite precision was swaying in a series of hairpin turns on his board. Up and down he wove in front of the house. She had to admit he could skate.

Chapter 6

"**W**hat's your name?" She had to screw up her courage to ask.

"Psi."

"S-i-g-h?"

"No, with a *p*. It's silent."

"What?"

"The *p*," the boy answered loftily. "Have you never heard of the 'silent *p*'? As in philanthropy. Or Prince Philip, defender of elephants?"

Cocky burst out laughing. "What are you talking about?"

"My name," answered the boy, tucking his skateboard under one arm and strolling along beside her quite as if he knew and liked her.

"Haven't you ever heard of the silent *p*?" he continued. "*P* before *n*, as in pneumonia and pneumatic. There is also the *p* before *t*, as in pterodactyl (a prehistoric vampire), ptarmigan (a grouse), ptomaine poisoning, and ptosis."

"Toes-ies?" Cocky laughed.

He looked at her with eyelids drooping sleepily. "In ptosis, the muscles of the eyelids don't work anymore."

Cocky stared at him fascinated. Isabel nosed a tree.

"And then," he continued, giving a little jump in the air that ended with a sweeping bow before her, "we come to the silent *p* before *s*. Pseudo, meaning fake" (he thrust one finger at her chest), "or psalms raised to God" (hands folded), "or psychopath" (his eyes rolled violently backward in his head), "psuffering from a psychosis." He straightened again. "And finally we come to my name. Psi. The twenty-third letter of the Greek alphabet. My name is Peter Simon Ilyich. They call me Si, man; and I have lengthened that to Psi, though hardly a soul can hear the difference in the sound. Psi, you see, with a silent *p*."

"Oh." Cocky had not followed one-tenth of this discourse. She didn't care. She knew his name was Si, or Sy, or Sigh, with somewhere a *p* that silently appeared. She also knew she had never met anyone like him before.

"Now, you are wondering about my last name, aren't you?"

Cocky shook her head, the thought never having crossed her mind.

"Ilyich," he continued. "Psi Ilyich. A silly itch. Ill he itches. There are a lot of them in Russia. Never joke about my name."

Cocky burst out laughing. She was so confused she didn't know his name. "Are you from around here?"

"No, I've come over for the hill." He gestured up toward R Street. "For skateboarding. I'm over the hill. Now come on, let's go get a newspaper."

"What for?"

"We have to see where the Secretary of State went off to."

"Oh. I could have asked Charlotte that."

"No, you couldn't," he answered, with the assurance that she found so interesting. "Then they would have known you knew he'd gone away."

"Well, if it's in the paper, won't they know we know?"

"They won't think to think," he said.

They bought a newspaper at People's Drugs, and returned to Cocky's house to read it in the sun on the front steps. Isabel sank gratefully to the ground.

Psi flipped the pages swiftly. He seemed to know what he

was looking for, and Cocky watched, impressed at his familiarity with every section.

"Here," he said. " 'Stinson to Saudi Arabia on peace mission ... The Secretary of State and entourage leave for Middle East today ... Bla-bla ... Three days of meetings before the upcoming Geneva peace talks ...' "

"What's that?" Cocky was relieved when Psi did not turn on her scornfully as if she ought to know.

"Oh, it's one *more* meeting of nations to make one *more* attempt at a peace settlement for the Middle East."

Cocky said nothing.

"There's always a war there. And now we're trying to make peace. The Geneva conference won't take place, though, for another three weeks," he continued. "First the United States is going to present our peace plan, and we hope to get both sides to accept it. And of course, as usual, they'll discuss the price of oil."

Cocky rocked back on her heels. "How do you know all this?"

"My father's very high up in the government," he whispered. "In the Agency, you know."

"The Agency?" Cocky was puzzled.

"The CIA." He pulled away impatiently. "Don't you know anything? Intelligence. Foreign operations. Spies."

"Oh." Cocky's father worked in the Navy. She knew only that he traveled a lot, and did something with contracts. It sounded a lot more interesting to have a father in the CIA.

In the next few days she learned that Psi's father had been a rodeo rider and a motorcycle stuntman in the movies, and then before becoming a CIA spy he'd been a brilliant physicist at MIT, which was a famous university in Boston. The more Cocky heard about him the more impressed she grew. Psi's mother was just as terrific. She was an actress in Hollywood.

"What movies was she in? Have I seen her?"

"Oh, a lot. I don't even know them all. Dozens of them,"

he answered. "She's not a big star," he added, "but she's always in movies. I'm going out to Hollywood soon with her." He strutted before Cocky, his hands deep in his jeans pockets. "I'm going out West when I'm sixteen. On a motorcycle, and I'll hitchhike around and maybe pick up some cowboy work and mess around with cars. And then I'll drift over to Hollywood and look up my Mom."

"Wow," Cocky said.

"Maybe I'll be a director." He shrugged. "She has a lot of contacts."

"I'm going to be an actress," Cocky interrupted, though it was the first time she'd ever thought of it. "Maybe you can direct me."

"Sure. Be glad to."

"Then you can introduce me to your mother."

Psi glanced at her, to see if she was teasing. With his father traveling all around the world, as a spy, he explained, and his mother acting in Hollywood, he wasn't in a position to make commitments for them.

Psi lived with an aunt just outside of Georgetown. The aunt worked as a cashier at Safeway, and the one time that Cocky saw her, she was hosing down the little patch of lawn in front of their house, wearing a bathrobe and bedroom slippers. She weighed about two hundred pounds, Cocky guessed, and had pink curlers in her hair.

Psi Ilyich. Silly itch. She couldn't see enough of him. If Cocky trotted through her day watching events unfold before her, Psi leaped, in his imagination, from crag to crag. He made things happen, and if details did not turn out as he liked, he reordered them in the telling until they did.

It was true that he sometimes noticed only a small part of the world around him. That amazed Cocky.

"Where were you?"

"Nowhere . . . just around."

"Well, what were you doing?"

"Nothing."

After a while she realized he was lost in dreams.

"Hey, did you see that man?"

"Where?" he asked.

"He almost knocked you down. He had a red tie and blue sneakers on."

"Oh, yeah?" Then twisting her words for fun: "Gee, a naked man. Red, white, and blue."

It made her laugh, how vacant he could be. At other times she found him so intense he almost seemed to tremble. It was as if there were a little wild animal inside him, straining to get out.

When Cocky thought about it, though, she felt sorry for Psi, what with both his parents gone. It was bad enough for her with just her father—She clipped the thought off short, cut clean as a fishing line. True, she reminded herself, Psi's parents were famous personalities, as he pointed out—two independent people who, though they loved each other deeply, were forced by their careers to live apart. But she wondered if he didn't miss them anyway.

"Shoot, no," he answered blithely. "I'm used to it. I don't need parents."

Apparently this was true, because Psi could handle any situation. He proved that with the DC 101 talent contest. The contest stood as a highwater mark that summer, and when it happened, Cocky bought a red spiral notebook to keep as a diary and "wrote down about the contest," as she put it, so that when she was old or lonely or depressed she could open her notebook and read about that moment of glory, her triumph with Psi.

Chapter 7

Psi had heard about the contest on the radio. It was a talent show to be held one Saturday morning outside the Key movie theater to advertise (a) the radio station DC 101, and (b) the Key Theater, and (c) the new movie playing there. The movie was called *Ekcentrik*. It was about all the crazy inventions in the world. It showed a grown man riding a three-inch-high bicycle and another man who invented a bicycle that changed into a canoe for crossing rivers, and then into a spiked tool for climbing telephone poles, and then into a tent for camping out. There were a lot of flapping flying-machines, shaped like bat, angel, or bird wings and made of everything from leather and canvas to feathers. They all crashed. Sometimes the man strapped himself into a leather harness with his wings on his back and jumped off a cliff and smashed into the ocean below. Sometimes he strapped it on his belly and ran down a gentle slope, while his wife jumped up and down in the background. None of the machines flew. One man climbed skyscrapers with his bare feet, and another played "Yankee Doodle" by pressing the palms of his hands together to make the air blurt out. Psi and Cocky nearly died laughing when they saw the film.

As for the contest, anyone could enter and do anything he wanted: sing, dance, do magic tricks. The person who got the most applause from the movie audience would win a hundred and one free records from DC 101.

Cocky and Psi were walking Isabel that Saturday morning when they heard the drum, a steady, deep throbbing. Isabel's head came up, ears pricked.

"That's it!" said Psi. "Let's go watch."

"Come on."

They raced down O Street, cut across Wisconsin and headed down the street, winding through the morning shoppers, dodging taxis and buses as they dashed across the street, heels pounding on the sidewalk until, flushed and breathless, they reached the theater. They slowed to a walk. The crowd was growing every moment. From its center, hidden from view, came the drumbeat. Psi jumped up and down at the edge of the crowd.

"I can't see."

"Wriggle," came Cocky's command; and the two disappeared, squirming between people's legs and under their elbows in their efforts to press forward.

Cocky's way was made more difficult by Isabel tangling her leash around the people's legs. "Excuse me," she said, unknotting the dog. "Sorry. Pardon me." Eventually she caught up to Psi.

A man, dressed entirely in white—white shirt, white suit, white vest, white buck shoes—was beating on a kettledrum. The pounding echoed right to her bones.

"Come one! Come all! Step right up!" A clown was dancing solemnly nearby and handing out balloons with the logo DC 101. The man in white set the drum behind him and picked up a microphone.

"Here it is, the chance of a lifetime," he shouted. "We at DC 101 are giving away absolutely free *one hundred and one* free records, and all you have to do is win them. It's the DC 101 Amateur Hour, and you'll see it tonight right here." He pronounced it *heee-aarr*, and he talked so loudly through the mike that his voice echoed against the bank across the street and bounced back at him, covering the next words of his sentence: "Right heee-aarr *(ear)* in this movie *(eee)* thee-a-ter *(rrr)*."

"Who today will be the lucky winner? One hundred and one best-selling hit-parade free records! Who will—"

"I will!" Cocky's hand shot up.

"There's a contestant!" He shouted approval. "Ladies and gentlemen, a round of *(oun if)* applause *(aws)*! What will it be? A song? A dance? A comedy routine?" He turned to Cocky. "All right, what are you going to do? *(wa oo)*?"

Cocky hardly hesitated. "An animal act," she said.

"Very good. An animal act," he repeated into the mike. "We don't have an animal act. That's terrific. Is this the animal?"

"Yes. This is Isabel. And a song," she added quickly. "I'll also sing a song," she explained, suddenly uncertain if an animal act would be enough.

"And a song." He scribbled on a pad. "Okay. You ready? Go ahead."

"Now?" Cocky was surprised. She had raised her hand so impulsively that she had no idea what the act would be. "I thought—"

"Wait a minute." Psi pushed forward. "Explain again how it works while I confer with my client."

Cocky looked at him gratefully.

The man gave a booming laugh into the microphone "Ha! ha!" that echoed back electronically amplified: *HA! HA!* "Very well. Each contestant tries out his act. If you qualify this morning, ladies and gentlemen, then you perform tonight before the entire theater audience, and the act that gets the most applause, that act, ladies and gentlemen, will win *one hundred and one* free records. Now we have a contestant here ready to try her hand for this stunning prize." He turned to Cocky. "Are you ready?"

Had Cocky known what lay ahead, she would never have continued. As it was, she felt a thrill of exhilaration. She felt as if she could do anything—walk a tightrope, lift a hundred pounds. She glanced around at the waiting crowd, and her face broke out in an engaging grin.

But it was Psi who grabbed the mike. "Ladies and gentlemen," he shouted. "The Cocky and Isabel Amazing Animal Act!" He strutted a few steps around the circle while the echo returned the tag ends of his words: *mal ak.*

"Clear a little circle here, a little space, please, so you can see this truly astonishing performance, the sight of your lives. Unforgettable . . ."

A ripple of laughter ran through the crowd, which shifted back a step to clear a space around the two young people and the basset hound. Isabel lay as usual on her stomach, gazing adoringly up at Cocky.

"Now, ladies and gentlemen, this world-famous animal tamer will ask anyone here—anyone at all *(all all)*—to make her dog stand up."

"Will what?"

"What did he say?"

"Who will volunteer to get this beautiful dog on her feet? Yes indeed, she does have feet. It's just that you can't see them now. Have I a volunteer?"

A man stepped forward. He was dressed in work clothes, and in one hand he held a Styrofoam cup of coffee. A long braid twisted down his back.

"Here, hold my cup," he said. Psi took the coffee. "I'll get him up. You ready?" He grinned around the circle and lifted both hands above his head triumphantly. "If I win, I get the records, right?" He winked at Cocky.

"Go to it, Mike," called a voice from the crowd.

Mike put one hand on either side of Isabel and heaved her to her feet. She looked at him with a puzzled air. "There!" He let go. Isabel slowly collapsed again.

The crowd burst into laughter.

"What happened?" said a man on the outer edge.

"I can't see."

The people on the outside of the circle pressed forward, stood on tiptoe, jumped from side to side in their efforts to see.

"Come on, dog," said Mike. "What's this dog's name?"

"Isabel."

"Come on, Isabel," he coaxed. "Stand up." Isabel looked wearily up at him.

"All right," Psi intervened quickly. "That's enough. We don't want this ferocious carnivore to bite. You could not keep her on her feet. Now watch Cocky Norton, world-famous animal tamer, *make her dog stand up (ug an up)*!"

The crowd pressed forward.

"I can't see."

"What's she doing?"

Cocky put one hand in her pocket. "Isabel," she called firmly, and at the same time pulled an Oreo from her pocket. "Stand *Up*!"

In a flash Isabel was on her feet, eyes glued to the cookie. Her ears pricked up. Her nose twitched. Her tongue lolled from her mouth.

"She's on her feet!" Psi roared into the microphone. "She did it *(idit idit)*! Ladies and gentlemen, the dog is up *(sup)*! And now Cocky Norton will make the dog lie down. Don't take your eyes off this animal. This is *it*, the big event. Note how she can make the dog *walk (awk)*, ladies and gentlemen. The dog is actually walking in a circle . . ."

Cocky slipped the cookie to Isabel's tongue. In a second it had disappeared. Quickly she commanded, "Lie down, Isabel."

Isabel licked her chops daintily and sank to the cement.

"There she is!" Psi's words were lost in laughter.

"What an act!"

"The dog lay down!"

"I like this act."

Psi held up one hand. He had to shout to be heard over the laughter, and almost every word pinged off the far building. "That is not all. Ladies and gentlemen, quiet, please. We have more. Cocky Norton, world-famous animal tamer, will now sing a duet with her dog. She will sing—" He glanced at Cocky.

" 'On Top of—' "

"Oh, yes. 'On Top of Old Smokey'! May we have your complete attention. Quiet, please. And-a one and-a two . . ."

"On top of *Oooooolllllllllllldd Smooooo-Keeeeeee.*" Cocky's voice rose. "All covered with *snooooowwwwww . . .*"

The rest was drowned by Isabel, who pulled herself up onto her two front feet, lifted her nose to the sky, and loosed a series of ungodly wails.

The crowd went crazy. Some people joined in the chorus. Psi himself was singing over the mike at the top of his lungs. The echoes bounded off the bank. People's voices and the dog's howls filled the warm summer air, competing against the blaring horns of buses and cars.

There is nothing like a crowd to draw a crowd. With every minute the crowd increased in size. Those in back were jumping up and down in a vain effort to see over the heads of those in front, and when they could not they began to push roughly forward.

"What's happening?"

"What is it?"

"Let me through."

"If you don't get your elbow out of my face—"

The din was deafening.

The crowd was growing unruly. Those in front fought back against the crush behind. Already at the outer fringes, people had spilled into the street, blocking traffic. They would not move. Cars and buses were stalled. They joined in a frantic honking as if noise alone would get their wheels to move. A boy, barefoot and without a shirt, leaped on the fender of a stalled car to see over the heads of the crowd, and when the driver opened his door, shouting and shaking his fist, the kid danced up onto the car roof, whooping like a baboon, until he suddenly stopped and began to point wildly down the street, shouting at the top of his voice. His words were lost in the noise, his gestures inexplicable, until above the chorus came the scream of an approaching squad car, *oooooOOOOOOOOOOOOOOaaaaaaaaaaaaaAAAAAAA.*

The boy jumped from the car and disappeared into the

seething mass of humanity. Only the clown's balloons could be seen bobbing in the air above the crowd. In the center Isabel, head thrown back, eyes tight shut, redoubled her efforts. She howled and howled.

Was it malice that led Psi to hold the microphone at Isabel's open mouth? He was dancing with excitement. Isabel's howls, amplified, rose and filled the street. The noise crashed over him like waves at the beach.

The man in white was laughing so hard that tears were pouring down his cheeks. He grabbed the mike from Psi.

"Ladies and gentlemen, please—" His voice too was drowned in the din. "May we have quiet, please. The police . . ."

Meanwhile Cocky, on her knees, held both hands protectively over Isabel's long, tender, silken ears.

"Come on, Cocky." Psi plucked her sleeve. "We'd better get out of here."

She looked up, puzzled.

"There's going to be a riot. Hurry."

Cocky pulled at Isabel's leash. "Come on, Isabel." But Isabel would not budge. Her rear stuck to the pavement as if by glue. She howled like a tired baby. The crowd was pushing and shoving, its mood shifting dangerously, for a crowd can quickly get out of control. It seethed around them. And then it exploded. One man hit another in the face. The blow was returned, and suddenly it seemed everyone was jostling and throwing punches.

The squad car pulled to a stop, its siren slowly dying.

"Come on, Isabel."

"Come on, Cocky. Quick!"

Two policemen leaped from the car. "All right. Get a move on. Break it up!"

"Reinforcements! Call for men," shouted one policeman to his buddy, who leaped to the car to radio for help.

When the police arrive, the press is never far behind. The community of Georgetown boasts a German TV station, and now a cameraman and reporter appeared on the scene, sprinting up M Street toward the riot. The cameraman, shoulders bent under fifty pounds of equipment, lumbered behind, but the motors of his cameras were churring. The reporter dived into the crowd, pushing his way roughly toward the center. In one hand he held a tape recorder, already turned on.

As he reached the center, he saw a patrolman bending over a young girl, who crouched beside a howling basset hound. With both hands she was covering the dog's ears, and she was looking up at the policeman with wide, startled eyes. Beside her a tall boy was hopping nervously from foot to foot.

Now the reporter's attention shifted to the police.

"All right, what's going on?" The cop pulled up his cartridge belt with heavy authority.

A man dressed all in white approached. He flicked an invisible speck off one immaculate arm and flashed a sparkling white smile at the cop. The reporter held his tape recorder in close.

"It's all right, officer. There's no trouble."

Cocky looked from one to the other.

"What's this about?" The patrolman's voice curled with anger.

"I'm Joe Gargero." The man in the white suit held out a calling card. "I'm head of publicity at DC 101. Do you listen to DC 101? And we're holding tryouts for our Amateur Hour. This girl and her dog were just doing their act."

"And that started a riot?" The policeman eyed Cocky. "What'd she do?"

"She made her dog stand up and lie down."

"She *what*?" He leaned forward angrily. "Listen, buddy, you take me for a fool? Kid around, I'll—"

"No, no—"

"—take you in for disrespect," he growled. The journalist leaned closer to record each word. "You telling me this crowd gathered to watch a *dawg* stand up?"

"Look, officer." Joe Gargero flashed his brilliant smile.

"It's a promotional gimmick, see, to promote DC 101 and also this fine new moviehouse and the movie that's just opening here." He motioned to the theater owner in the shadow of the building. "Nate, come over here."

"Well, not here, you ain't," the policeman interrupted. "Not on the public streets. You get someplace else for your rehearsals."

"They aren't rehearsals. They're—"

The crowd boiled around them, swirling with increasing anger.

"You got a license for a public rally?"

"License?" His smile vanished. "But this isn't a rally."

"I can pull you in for inciting to riot . . . parading without a permit . . ."

"Officer, I—"

". . . obstructing the sidewalk."

"Listen, none of that is true. All we're—"

"You want I should book you for resisting arrest?" The policeman was not smiling. He turned to Cocky and Isabel, who was still howling at his feet. "Get that mutt outa here. I can't hear a word."

"Officer, I—"

"All right, everyone." He turned to the crowd. "If you're going to stand here, you got to keep moving."

Two more squad cars pulled up. Five policemen were pressing the crowd back, to break it up. Yet still no one left. The crowd jostled, pushed. The TV cameraman had reached the reporter's side. He focused the camera first on Cocky and Isabel, then on the policemen handling the crowd, finally on Psi, the man in white, the clown with his balloons.

The reporter now hunkered down beside Cocky. "What happened?" He thrust out the mike. "Can you tell us what happened?"

"It's a goddam riot!" shouted the policeman to his partner. "Get that traffic moving. Get 'em outa here!"

But it was not until a park policeman rode up on a big black horse that the crowd began to melt.

42

"George!" yelled Cocky. Her voice was too thin to be heard above the din.

George urged Leggins into the middle of the crowd. Patiently the horse pushed forward, stepping slowly along as people moved aside for him. And wherever the big horse had passed, the crowd broke up into smaller and smaller units.

"Get a move on," shouted the police. "Come on, break it up!"

Another patrolman was blowing his whistle in the street. "Move it!" he shouted. "Move your butt!"

Slowly the crowd broke apart. What had been a single cohesive mass dissolved first into smaller groups, then into twos and threes, and finally into isolated individuals who found themselves suddenly standing alone on the sidewalk. Then they looked around embarrassed, as if they were just waking up, and sheepishly, lest someone they knew see them there, they began to hurry off.

Slowly traffic eased forward. Only a small cluster remained: the clown with his balloons, looking the worse for being pressed by the mob, the man in dazzling white, the girl and boy hovering over their dog. The cameraman had unstrapped his heavy camera and set it at his feet. He leaned in boredom against the building to light a cigarette. The man in white spread his hands before the two cops, shrugging his shoulders in apology and all the time talking as fast as he could and flashing his brilliant smile from one to the other. The two officers stared at him stolidly. One hooked his thumbs into his gun belt and rocked back on his heels; after a moment the other hurried to the squad car to answer the crackling static that screamed from the radio.

The park policeman rode back up the street.

"George!" shouted Cocky. He turned in the saddle, and Cocky was struck by how military he looked in his blue uniform and the black saddle blanket embroidered with the initials NPS.

"Hey, what are you doing here?" He leaned down to speak to her.

"Oh, George, you were wonderful!" she continued happily. "You and Leggins both."

"What happened?" he asked.

"I don't know. We were just trying out for a talent contest, and Psi— He's my friend over there." She turned and motioned to him. "Psi, this is George. I guess none of it would have happened without Psi," she said proudly. "He did it all."

Psi looked at her in astonishment. "What do you mean?"

"No, you did," she said with generous enthusiasm. "You were great."

"Well, it's nothing to be proud of." George straightened, frowning. "Starting a riot." He nodded to Psi. "I'll remember you." He turned Leggins then, nodded to Cocky, and trotted up the street. Cocky was left looking after him, her mouth open in surprise.

Psi turned to her. "What'd you say that for?"

"I'm sorry. I thought—"

"Well, don't think!"

Cocky felt her anger rise to match his own.

The officer at her side closed his ticket book, held up one warning hand, and sauntered slowly to his partner in the car. He leaned on the hood of the car, surveying the street—his street. Then he dropped into the front seat and closed the door.

Only the man in white remained on the sidewalk. He was talking in a low voice to his friend the theater owner. The clown was sitting in the shade of the theater lobby. Isabel lay exhausted on the sidewalk. Cocky looked over at Psi. He returned her look, shrugged, and then, to her relief, grinned. They were friends again.

"Do you think we won?"

"Let's ask."

They approached the two men.

"Oho!" said the man in white, breaking into a wide grin. "Well, you two certainly stirred up a storm."

"Did we win?" asked Cocky.

"Win what?"

"A hundred and one free records."

He laughed. "No, but you sure won the chance to compete tonight. Come back at eight and we'll run through your dog act again inside the theater for the audience." He winked. "You got a great chance to win."

"Oh, but wait." The words burst out almost like a sob. "I can't come back tonight."

"You can't?"

"She's not my dog. She belongs to the Secretary of State. I can't take her out at night."

"The Secretary of State! Does she really?" He looked down at Isabel, impressed. "Well, she sure is a terrific dog, and you've got a fantastic act there. I'll never see the like of that again," he laughed.

"We can't win them now?"

"I'm sorry, honey. We can't. We can't even stay here now to have the rest of the tryouts."

"Oh. I'm sorry if we destroyed your publicity."

"Destroy my publicity!" He was amazed. "Why, little lady, you've just given us enough publicity to last a month! We've got the whole thing on tape. Now, we'll just run it over the radio all day to advertise our Amateur Hour. If you go home, you can hear it in an hour." He winked again. "You'll be famous. We'll even announce the dog is Isabel, belonging to the Secretary of State." He laughed again, a deep belly laugh, and elbowed his friend in the ribs.

"So we don't get any records?" Her voice was pathetic.

The two men looked at each other. "We can't give you that, honey, unless you win tonight."

"Oh. Well. . . ."

"Wait." The theater owner spoke for the first time. "That was a great performance you two put on. I'm going to give you something. I want you to have two free passes for a year to my movie theater. Okay? You can come in anytime."

Cocky glanced at Psi. "Oh, yes."

"Wait here a minute. I'll just write it up for you."

A few minutes later he reappeared from the ticket booth carrying a metallic silver card.

" 'Good for two,' " read Cocky, " 'for one year from—' Oh, thank you." Her eyes sparkled.

"Good-bye, dog," the man in white called after them. "Give my regards to the Secretary of State."

Cocky and Psi were ecstatic. They danced up the street, turning the pass to catch the light from its shiny metal surface and talking excitedly.

"You were wonderful," said Cocky.

"Yes, but it was your idea," he returned modestly. "And you really did it well."

"Did you see that crowd?"

"Were you scared?"

It was then that Psi felt the touch on his shoulder. He turned to face a dark, plump man with a wart on his chin. The man was panting, as if breathless from a run.

"Excuse me." His black eyes flicked from one to the other restlessly. "I couldn't help but overhear. Does your dog really belong to the Secretary of State?"

Cocky stared at him transfixed.

"She really does," Psi answered proudly. "Cocky's the official dogwalker."

"Well, well." His dark eyes hovered on Cocky, then flashed to the dog. His tongue flicked like a lizard's across his lips—slipped, and was gone. "Such a talented dog." He bent to pat Isabel. "And so well behaved. Well, well." He pulled from his breast pocket a large white handkerchief and delicately wiped his hand where he had touched the dog. "Well, good day." He nodded to them both. "Yes, a lovely dog."

Then he was hurrying down the street, leaving Cocky and Psi to look after him in astonishment.

"Psi," whispered Cocky unhappily, "I wish you hadn't said that."

"Why?"

"Because that was the man," she said miserably, "who took the briefcase from the Secretary of State."

Chapter 8

In the next few weeks Cocky and Psi were inseparable. The days passed in a golden blur of light and laughter, and what did it matter that Cocky's mother seemed more nervous than ever? She smeared her skin with cocoa butter and sunburned to a chocolate brown, oiling and broiling herself in the back garden or at the Hilton Hotel tennis club. And what did it matter if she drank with Mrs. Barr every evening until their voices grew shrill and loud, or that sometimes her mother would go out at night, her eyelids covered with blue makeup, her mouth a slash of red, and that she would return with her friends, reeling with laughter and waking Cocky up with their hiccups and giggling? What did it matter if Cocky's father stayed away week after week without phoning?

But it did matter. Cocky was humiliated when her mother dyed her hair platinum, then red, then back to frosted blond.

"What's wrong with just plain brown?" she raged. "I liked it brown. It was pretty when it was—"

"Cocky!"

"Dad's going to blow his stack when he sees—"

"Katharine Anne Norton!" Her mother turned on her viciously. "When are you going to grow up? You know perfectly well your fa—"

But Cocky clapped both hands over her ears and shouted above her words. "I know! I know! All right!"

"What's the matter with you, anyway?"

"I can't stand it, that's what. Now you'll go back to school in the fall with all that yellow hair. Or red! It looks awful!"

"Well, lucky for you, Cocky Norton, that I teach at a different school from yours, and you won't have to look at me."

"You're a math teacher!" Cocky stamped her foot. "You're supposed—"

"Don't you classify me! 'You're a mother!' 'You're a math teacher!' So what? A math teacher can't color her hair, I suppose? Besides," she added, fluffing her short curls before the hallway mirror, "I thought it looked kind of sexy."

"Oh, Mother!"

"What's the matter with you, Cocky? You want to stay a child forever? You have to—"

"Grow up!" Cocky snapped the words sarcastically. "Don't I know? It's all you talk about. Well, I just don't care to smear makeup all over my eyes and giggle about boys, if that's what growing up's about." She lurched awkwardly across the hall. "I won't do it."

"I can't imagine why not." Her mother turned from the mirror, her voice taking on the superior tone that made Cocky fume. "You certainly think enough about one boy." Cocky said nothing. "You're never home anymore. What do you two do all day, anyway?"

"Nothing. We play."

"Don't look away like that. I have a perfect right to know. You're a very pretty girl now, and frankly we don't know the first thing about that boy."

"Oh, Mother!"

"I mean it. Who are his parents, anyway? Where's he from? That's what I want to know."

"For heaven's sake! Who cares?"

"And why does he hang around this neighborhood? Doesn't he have any friends?"

"Mother!"

"Well, you know I don't like you to—"

"Oh, leave me alone!"

"Cocky!" Her mother caught her arm as she spun toward the door. "Come on, honey." Her voice softened. "Let's not fight. You act so strange with me now. As if you're ashamed of me. You won't go to the pool with me. Or play tennis. We used to have good times, remember?"

Cocky shrugged and turned aside. She could not meet her mother's eyes.

"You can't stay home now for a minute. You're always with that boy. If it weren't for food, I don't think you'd bother to come home at all."

"You should talk." It was an undertone, delivered under her breath, but her mother caught the words and her temper flared in hurt response.

"Sure, I go out occasionally," she exploded. "My God! I wish it were more often! What's here? An empty house? Look, I'm going through a rough time right now. It's not as if you're any help. You make no effort to see my side of things. Well, just you wait, Cocky Norton. Someday you'll find out what it's like."

"I've gotta go," said Cocky coldly. "Psi's waiting."

"Psi's waiting. Psi's always waiting. Look, just be careful, that's all I can say. Just you watch your step."

"I don't even know what you're talking about!" Cocky spun around, her eyes filling with passionate tears.

"Oh, honey." Her mother was stricken with remorse. "Hey, come on. Let's not fight. I like him, Cocky, really I do." She hugged Cocky to her. "Come on." She tucked one hand under Cocky's chin. "Smile?"

Cocky smiled weakly and returned the squeeze. "I'm sorry, Mom."

"Listen, come on over to the pool with me today, you and Psi. You can both come. Mitsi Barr wants to talk about my changing jobs. I can't imagine why. You want to?"

"Maybe tomorrow, okay?" Cocky shifted her feet uneasily. She didn't want to see Mrs. Barr or share her time with Psi.

When he was with her, everything seemed all right. Then an hour passed like ten minutes; and after he left, his presence floated before her. His walk, the turn of his head, played before her eyes for hours. Every evening after finishing work at Safeway, he was at her house, and they did not part until dusk, when voices seemed to ring more clearly than in the moist white heat of day. He taught her mumblety-peg with his jackknife. They walked along the canal with the muleteers, guiding the mules that drew the barges for the tourist rides. They skipped stones on the river and climbed trees. But their favorite sport was skateboarding. Psi taught Cocky about trucks and wheelies, how to "click-clack," slalom, and "walk the dog." Or they practiced barrel jumps. Cocky crouched on the ground, knees and elbows tucked froglike under her. Her skateboard stood against her side as a shield. Psi took off from up the hill, and, gaining speed as he roared straight at her, slammed his board into her shield, leaped over her, and landed running on the other side. Sometimes he practiced standing on his hands skating on the board, and what he was working toward was a barrel jump over Cocky in which he landed on another skateboard after his leap.

"Cocky, come on in!" her mother called. "Are you still out there? It's nearly nine o'clock."

"I've got to go," she said. By then it was so dark she could barely see his face.

"Just one more trick."

"I'm coming—" she called back to her mother. She could never tear herself away. It was always just one more stunt, one more "rad." Their shoulders brushed lightly in the dusk. Once she reached out, caught a firefly. "Here," she said. "A present."

He took it in his two cupped hands, his fingers brushing hers. His touch was gentle. "Don't hurt it." She leaned in toward him.

"Cocky! Come inside this minute!" Her mother was

silhouetted in the doorway against the yellow light. "Psi, will you please go home," she laughed. "She'll be here in the morning."

"Good night." One foot spun him down the sidewalk.

"Good night."

"Bye," Cocky called after him. "See you tomorrow!" Her voice was thin in the darkness. How was it possible for night to come so fast?

Far down the street, lost in the rumble of wheels, Psi lifted one hand high above his head. He opened his fist and, head thrown back, watched the tiny burst of light against his palm, then blackness. An instant later a firefly flickered high in the air behind him. By then Cocky had already gone inside, his eyes shining before her, his voice echoing in her ears.

She thought that nothing could interfere with such a friendship, and in her fierce loyalty she bravely bore her mother's teasing.

"I've *neeeev-er* been in love before," her mother caroled. Or, "It must be *luv* cuz jam don't shake like that!"

Cocky would recoil in embarrassment. "Oh, Mother!"

"Dancing in the *daarrrk* . . . ," her mother would sing, clasping a sofa pillow tightly to her chest and twirling around the living room. "Cocky's in love," she confided to Mrs. Barr, who grinned knowledgeably.

Cocky would race from the house, angry and confused. There was a savagery to her mother's teasing, as if she were annoyed with Cocky; or as if being in love—or even loving another person—were a matter not of joy, but of shame. At times like that Cocky was glad her father was away. Being teased by one parent was enough.

But Psi had to put up with even more. One morning as he was unpacking cartons of cabbages at the Safeway, Joel Ray and his friend Jones burst through the doors from the front of the store. They were doubled over laughing, and they punched each other on the shoulder and careened against the boxes.

"Oh, geesus," Jones laughed. "It's too much."

"I *love* it!"

"D'ja see his face?"

"What's happened?" Psi grinned shyly.

"Oh, we was just horsin' around," Jones said. "Joel Ray here's showing off pictures of his girl friend. Aincha, Joel Ray?" And the two boys collapsed on the cement floor cackling.

"Let's see." Psi was curious.

"Oh, no." Joel Ray snatched away his hand. "You're too young."

"He's too young," echoed Jones, who had his own car. "You gotta be old enough to drive."

"You gotta be old enough to *drive*," emphasized Joel Ray. "You ever drive, man?"

"What?"

"Hey, skater." Jones put one arm around Psi's shoulder with an intimate whisper: "You got a girl?"

"Sure I've got a girl." Psi puffed his chest and swaggered back to his cardboard cartons. The other two followed behind. "You should *see* my girl."

"See, what I tell you?" Joel Ray said. "Did'n I say he'd have a girl? He's jive, man. The skate man. *Coo-ool.*"

"You think I don't know nothin'?" Psi allowed with a grin. He slit a carton skillfully with one clean stroke of his knife.

"What's she like, man? She pretty?" He jabbed Psi's shoulder playfully with one fist, to which he responded by silently drawing a girl's shapely figure in the air with his hands. Both boys whistled.

"Um-hum!"

"Ain' he the sly one, though?" Joel Ray laughed in admiration.

"Hey, skater! I bet you's a fiend with the girls. A regular fiend."

"Oh, them Saturday nights!" called Jones. He lay on his back, kicking his heels in the air. "I cain wait fo Sat'day nights."

"You cain wait. Nothin' to wait for, with you."

"Shee-it, man."

"Shoot. Skater'll do better'n you. You ain' even *got* no girl." At which the two boys fell wrestling to the floor.

Psi rolled the cart piled with vegetables through the double doors to the front of the store. He was just as glad to have an excuse to leave, not caring to be the butt of their humor any longer. At the same time he rather liked the image he had painted of himself and as the hours wore on he elaborated to them on the beauty, skills, and virtues of his girl. All day he strutted a little taller as he worked, and when Jones offered him a cigarette during a break, he took a puff, blew the smoke up toward the ceiling, and returned the stub with a satisfied nod.

It never entered his head that Cocky would decide to come up to the Safeway with Isabel, and when he got the word the very next day, that a girl and her hound were out back asking for him, he visibly blanched.

"Who?" he asked.

"Ah don' know, man. Some lil' chickadee, like, and a big ol' houn' dog."

Psi stepped outside with reluctant steps. Jones and Joel Ray followed along behind.

"Is *that* your girl?" Jones snickered, and collapsed up against Joel Ray. Psi shot him a black look.

"Hi," said Cocky with a big cheerful smile. "I thought I'd come see where you work."

"Yeah."

She leaned toward him, whispering confidingly. "Do you think you can get a bone from the butcher for Isabel?"

Psi bent to pat the basset, who responded with a quick slap of her tongue across his mouth, her tail wagging. "Sure," he said coolly. "Wait a second."

He was glad to hurry on the errand, and hardly noticed that Joel Ray and Jones were sauntering toward Cocky.

"Hi," said Jones.

"Hello," Cocky looked up, bright eyes sparkling.

"You a friend of Psi's, huh?"

"Yeah." She cast her eyes down shyly, and the two boys exchanged a knowing glance.

"Hey, what you call that dog?" asked Jones.

"It's a basset."

"Basset," repeated Jones. "If that ain' the funniest-lookin' animal."

"You know him long?"

"Who? The dog?"

"No, the skater."

"Psi," Joel Ray explained, seeing her uncomprehending look. "We calls him the skater, cuz he's always on top of that board of his."

"Oh, yeah. We're real friends. We're always together." She stood up proudly. "We're a *team*!"

They both burst out laughing, as Cocky looked from one to the other in astonishment. She could not imagine what she'd said that was so funny, or why when Psi returned with a package wrapped in brown paper he thrust it roughly at her. "Here." He scowled at the two boys. "I gotta go."

"Hey, skater," Jones called out.

"Hey, man." Joel Ray raced after him, laughing. "Where you goin'? Don' you wanna talk to your girl friend, man?"

Cocky looked after them, her mouth open. She did not know what to make of Psi's rigid back, the quick sidewise toss of his head, or the fact that Jones and Joel Ray burst into raucous laughter and disappeared through the double doors, tussling behind Psi and taunting, "That's your girl friend, right? We right about your girl?"

"Come on, Isabel." She turned away, confused. She felt uncomfortable. "At least you got a bone. Smell it? Yum-yum. Come on, that's right. Jump for it." She pushed the disconcerting scene out of her mind.

But to Psi it was only the beginning, for after that the boys took every opportunity to torment him. It wasn't hard. Jones had his own car, a rusting, tailpipe-dragging Plymouth with an old-fashioned necker's knob on the steering wheel. He had only to see Psi crossing the parking lot and he'd lean out the broken window and shout, "Hey, skater, how'd you make out with your girl last night?"

Psi would force a smile. "How're you doing?" he'd respond, cool as John Wayne; but the catcalls made him squirm with shame.

And so one Saturday morning when he was skating over to Cocky's house to help her walk Isabel and the gang of small kids leaped out, taunting him, their words slashed at him like a whip. The children were only six or seven, and some could have been younger still: a flock of ducklings, all short, stubby legs and treble laughs. They dashed out from the archway of a house, chanting:

Psi and Cocky sitting in a tree
K-I-S-S-I-N-G
First comes love
Then comes marriage
Then comes Psi with a **BABY CARRIAGE!**

It was the last straw. Psi swerved back toward the children. The blood was pounding in his ears, his hands began to shake, and to his horror he felt tears prickling at his eyes—the purest physical reaction from his surge of rage, but to him it appeared a demonstration of weakness. With a dreadful scream, he bore down on the children, who fled with squeals of fear and delight.

Psi and Cocky sitting in a tree . . .

They scattered like swallows, twittering at their joke. In a moment Psi was left alone, his heart racing. He felt dirtied by the song. A monkey in a tree, k-i-s-s-i-n-g. He felt small and exposed. And what was most awful, he knew, was that the ridicule was deserved. He did hang around Cocky. Moreover, she wasn't a pin-up playmate that a man could boast about to a buddy, punching him on the upper arm and leering, "Yeah, man." She was just a shabby kid.

He pumped his skateboard up the steep hill toward R Street and Montrose Park. His lips curled back. His head jerked to one side. As the pitch of the hill slowed him down, he snatched the skateboard from underfoot and began to run. He raced to the top of the hill, then deep into the park, to drop finally to the ground, gasping for air. He rolled over and over on the grass in rage, until at last, his anger spent, he sprawled on his back, spread-eagled under the sky.

He threw one arm across his face and gave a vicious twist, to wipe his eyes in secret. How horrible to cry! He blinked and opened his eyes. Above him the white clouds puffed across the vault of the sky. It had been years since he had lain on his back watching clouds. The sun was warm. Gradually the tension drained out of his back and legs. He wiped his mouth with the back of his hand. He felt exhausted, and at the same time a great sorrow was welling up in him, like a huge bubble filling his chest. He felt he would choke. In another moment it would burst, and Peter Simon Ilyich would drown in a river of—He sprang to his feet, cursing under his breath. "Sorry for yourself. You stupid ass."

Moments later Psi was striding down the hillside toward the woods. He glared over at the playground from which rose the shrill shrieks of little children's joy; then he plunged down the hill and into the woods.

Chapter 9

Cocky waited on her front steps for Psi. She sat, arms circling her knees and filled with a sweet anticipation. A small green hairy caterpillar crawled slowly across the stone step beside her. She put one finger in its way. The caterpillar reared up, startled, and threw itself backward. Another finger barred its way. It had no choice but to climb the smooth pink hand. The caterpillar was a pale, translucent green. Its bristles glistened in the light. Cocky looked up the street for Psi. Since they had first met, he had never missed a Saturday morning of dogwalking with her, and never had he been late. She transferred the caterpillar gently to a leaf. She lingered on her block as long as she could, and when she finally traced her steps toward the Stinsons', she turned often to look over her shoulder for Psi. But he did not appear. It occurred to her that he might be waiting at Isabel's. With a light heart she broke into a run.

But he was not there either.

That day her walk with Isabel seemed dull. Psi did not appear all day, and neither did he come around the following morning. On the third, Cocky saw him in the distance. She called out, "Psi!" Did he see her? She thought she saw him turn his head, but in another moment he had disappeared.

She was hurt.

Once she telephoned his house, but when his aunt answered, she found herself stricken with shyness. She could not speak.

"Hello?" said the aunt to the silent telephone. "Hello?"

Cocky threw the receiver down. Then she sat glowering at the instrument until her mother came into the room.

"There you are. What are you doing?"

"Nothing." She rose.

"Good heavens, stand up straight. What's the matter with you, anyway? Are you sick?"

"I feel fine. Leave me alone," she cried, and lunged out the door. She walked and walked. She wished Liza were around. She wondered if she would see Psi on the street, and then if she should wait at home for him to telephone. She walked all the way to his block, but no sooner got there than she ran away, lest he should find her there. One moment she forgave him everything, convinced that something terrible had happened to him. The next moment she was filled with anger: the least he could do was telephone.

She had no control over her feelings. She sat in the shade hugging her knees and lost in misery.

Later Cocky was walking absently along the street, watching Isabel. She kicked a stone along the sidewalk, then just stopped and stood in the dull white heat, staring off at nothing. Huge sighs filled her chest.

Then she heard the wheels. She turned and there he was slaloming toward her, head up, arms spread like wings. Her heart gave a leap and the sun was back in the sky, glittering on his helmet. He swung toward her, his smile flashing.

How strange is the human heart! Why Cocky behaved as she did she could never explain, and afterward she kicked herself for it and replayed the scene in her memory again and again in other ways. He swept toward her, his face lit by a beautiful smile—and Cocky turned away.

His face fell. He gave a grunt, "Hmph," and instead of stopping he skidded off to the far side of the street. Instantly Cocky was sorry.

There was a ghastly pause. She stared deliberately at Isabel, not daring to look up, though she could hear the churring of his wheels. She wanted to call out to him, but could not speak.

Out of the corner of her eye she watched him turn and glide. He did not look at her. Every circle of his skateboard took him farther away, so that with each second it grew harder to call across that space. The pause lengthened. She looked up. He slalomed down the street . . . and was gone.

Cocky was horror-struck. She looked after him helplessly.

Then she was swept by hurt and anger. "Well, if he's going to be *that* way," she murmured to Isabel, jerking the leash. "Come on, you. It's time to go home." She had never spoken harshly to Isabel before.

Later she said, "Who cares, anyway?" Isabel glanced over one shoulder inquisitively. "Certainly *I* don't," she finished as they reached Isabel's steps. Again Isabel looked up at Cocky expectantly. She was hoping for a longer walk.

"Come on, Isabel." Cocky tugged the leash impatiently. "Hurry up." With a sigh Isabel started up the steps. Her sadness touched Cocky. "Oh, Isabel, I'm sorry." She brushed her cheek against the dog's. "I'll give you a long walk this afternoon. I promise."

That afternoon Cocky twisted through the back alleys of Georgetown, exploring with an intensity and determined lack of enjoyment that can only be attributed to pain. For the first time she understood what such words as "heartache" meant. She felt a physical wrenching as if her heart were being twisted inside her chest like a rag. She did not know when she would see Psi again, and she had only herself to blame. She was too proud to go look for him, and if she did see him she wasn't sure what she would say.

By the time she found herself back in the Stinsons' block, her mood had worked around from self-pitying to hopping mad. She was raring for a fight. It was then that she remembered the tent in the Stinson garden. When she had told Psi about it, he had suggested their sneaking in together to inspect it. She thought how jealous he would be if she did it all alone.

The Secretary of State was in Geneva at the peace conference. The Secret Service would be gone . . .

She turned up the Stinson alley, walking with a furtive tread. It took her almost no time at all to find a point of entry. A garbage can moved over several feet . . . a step . . . the smallest jump, and Cocky was crouching on top of the fence. Beneath her was the L-shaped garden with its petunias and climbing roses. It was bigger than she had remembered. Her eyes scanned the tent. All was still. The house looked closed up, dead, with each window blinded by shutters or heavy draperies.

A bird whistled in the cherry tree. A soft breeze stirred the leaves. Otherwise nothing moved. She was right, she thought: everyone was away.

Silently she jumped to the grass.

She crossed the lawn in long running steps and had just reached the tent when Isabel leaped out with a joyous bark, tail whipping in circles above her back. Cocky's heart knocked so hard she almost choked.

"*Shh*, Isabel." She dropped to one knee beside the dog and held her finger to her lips. Then, quickly, she ducked under the tent flap—and froze!

A man was watching her. In his hand, pointing straight at her, was a small black revolver. Beside him in a green upholstered garden chair sat the Secretary of State.

Chapter 10

For a long moment no one spoke. Then the Secretary of State said, "Well, you'd better come in out of the light. You can be seen from there."

She flushed, took one step forward, and stopped, eyes held by the metallic glitter of the gun.

"I—I'm—"

Slowly the agent lifted the nose of the revolver. It pointed at her chest . . . her mouth . . . her eyes. At moments of intense excitement the mind registers details with startling clarity. Cocky noticed that the black mouth of the pistol formed a perfect O. She noticed that the man's string tie was held by an oval turquoise clasp.

"It's all right, Buck." The Secretary of State waved one hand. "You can go."

"Are you sure?"

"Stay just outside. Watch for—you know."

"Sir—" Buck was clearly worried.

"I'm perfectly all right." He never took his eyes off Cocky.

"Okay, but take this," the agent said miserably. He handed the Secretary of State the revolver and slipped under the tent flap.

The two were left alone. Cocky shifted uneasily. She could not keep her eyes off the revolver. The Secretary of State wore slate-gray slacks that matched the slate floor, and his legs were crossed casually at the knee. He was leaning back in the chair as if at ease, and he watched her with an amused smile.

"So. Who are you? An angel?"

"What?"

"I was just praying for an angel of the Lord, when you came over the fence."

"My mother says I'm a devil," Cocky answered literally.

"Well, that's my luck." He gave a bitter laugh and turned the pistol sidewise, holding it across his lap with both hands. Still he surveyed her up and down.

"I see that Isabel knows you." His voice was hard as he nodded at the dog, sitting, tail thumping, at her feet.

"Yes. I'm really sorry. I didn't mean any— I thought you were away." The words tumbled out of her mouth. "I wanted to see inside the tent."

"That's not what I asked you," he said severely. "Why does my dog know you?"

"I walk her," answered Cocky, bending to rub Isabel's stomach. Her hands were shaking from the tension and terror. "That's my job," she rattled on. "I'm your dogwalker, and I saw your tent one day. I thought everyone was away and I could just come peek inside. I wasn't going to touch anything, but I'd read in the papers where you were away."

The Secretary of State lay the revolver on a pile of papers that covered the glass table beside him.

"Well, well." He looked at Cocky. "And what am I going to do now?" He closed his eyes wearily, and for a moment his face sagged. He looked like an old and tired man.

Cocky shifted uneasily from foot to foot. She would have given anything to be someplace else. She glanced furtively around. The tent was a circular structure, cool and private. The roof rose in soft folds to a high peak, and the sunlight streamed through the broad yellow and white stripes, casting bands of light across the green-flowered furniture.

"You may as well sit down," said the Secretary of State, gesturing to a chair. "Do you like it?"

"Oh, it's beautiful." She settled on the edge of a chair, conscious of his unremitting gaze. His brows were reddish-brown and shaggy, hanging over his eyes. She stared back at the older man and suddenly she was filled with anger.

"I thought you were in Geneva," she said. "Everyone in the whole world thinks you're in Geneva. Making peace." She became increasingly agitated. Her voice was accusatory. "Why aren't you there? That's where you belong. Not here, hiding in your own garden. Why aren't you working to make peace?"

She stopped, appalled at her outburst, but the Secretary of State threw back his head with a laugh. It was just a single sound, a quick sharp bark—and replaced by a smile of illimitable sorrow.

"Is that right?" he said. "Is that where I should be? I was expecting the President to come bawl me out. Has he sent you to tell me how to make peace in the Middle East?"

Under other conditions Cocky would have shrunk under such scorn, but she had undergone three days of fevered emotions and her feelings were close to the surface.

"Has he sent you to tell me what to do?"

"If you want." Her eyes flashed. "What do you need to know?"

He threw back his head again and laughed out loud. "All right." He leaned forward. "Devil or angel. Name a problem. I have a hundred problems. All deal in death. Name a field . . . Yes, animals. You like animals. All right, here's one. Tell me how to solve the problem of the whales." He stood up and paced to the tent flap, gave a nod to Buck, and threw himself back into his chair.

"You ready? There is something called the International Whaling Commission. One of its duties is to put a limit to the number of whales that each nation can hunt and kill, because we hunt the whales now with huge factory ships, as big as football fields, and we harpoon them with big guns mounted on the decks of these swift vessels, ships so fast they can outdistance any mammal in the sea. We run them to exhaustion. And when they come up for air—did you know that whales breathe air, like you and me?—then they are shot by a cannon on the deck of the ship. So the whales are being destroyed at such a rate we're afraid this order of creatures will soon be extinct." Again he closed his eyes. "They've never harmed any living creature. They're the gentlest . . ."

Cocky squirmed back into her chair. "Why do we hunt them?"

He shrugged. "We make things from them. Margarine, fine machine oils, fertilizer, cat food. The Japanese eat the meat. Some parts are used for perfume."

"Oh." It was a sigh, barely audible in the tent.

"So we—mankind—is hunting the whales to extinction. Already we're afraid we've killed too many of certain kinds. The blues. The humpbacks. Are you shocked?"

She looked away.

"Now, here's the problem. The International Whaling Commission has put strict limits on the numbers that each nation can kill. This is something that we in the United States have been pushing for for a long time. And finally all the Commission countries have agreed. Only *now*"—he leaned forward, rubbing his hands together—"we find that the Eskimos up in Alaska—Americans, just like us—say that they will not abide by the quota. Because they hunt whales to live. And if the Eskimos break the agreement, then the Russians and Japanese and other nations in the Commission will too; and we'll have lost everything we fought for."

"But can't the Eskimos eat something else?" asked Cocky. "Can't we ship them canned goods?"

"Ah, but they like whale. And they've always hunted whale. And who would pay for the canned goods? And anyway, it's a matter of pride with the Eskimos, because they prove their manhood by killing the whales. The difference, of course, is that instead of using spears as in the old days, they use our modern instruments of death."

"The heavy guns?"

"With grenades inside. They hit the whale and it explodes inside."

Cocky felt sick. "How many whales do they need to kill each year to survive?"

"Not so many. But, you see, since they use the explosives, sometimes the whales escape, and then they die later anyway out in the deep water and can't be used for food. A pretty story, don't you think? You see, it's a question of different cultures. Killing whales is how the young men prove themselves. That's their heritage, and we can't just take it away. But if we don't . . . So tell me now, what are we to do?"

"I think," Cocky said slowly, "that perhaps the Eskimos should be allowed to hunt and kill as many whales as they want."

"You do?"

"They should be free from the agreement," she continued. "So long as they use the same weapons they used in the past. Since the hunt itself is the important part, or anyway as important as the kill—to show their skill, I mean—then they should be able to kill as many whales as they want. But if they are going to use the white man's guns and grenades, then they must abide by the white man's rules. And I think we should also send them other food, so they—"

The Secretary of State clapped both hands on his knees. "The wisdom of Solomon," he declared. But his mouth turned down at the corners so that Cocky could not tell whether he was making fun of her or not.

She flushed and looked away. When he stopped laughing he reached for his half-spectacles on the table beside him (and again she glanced at the ugly chunky gun). He settled them on his nose and, chin lowered, peered over the glasses at her.

"Now, the Middle East," he said. "The whales are an annoying problem, but, you see, the whales are mute, pathetic creatures, at the mercy of man, and if they become extinct their demise represents no loss to us." His voice was light, but his eyes were clouded. "A whale cannot surprise us with a nuclear attack. But man's inhumanity to man . . . ah, that's a different thing. We call ourselves human, little angel, and out of that we build this word *humane*, by which we mean compassionate and kind. But only man kills his own kind. Did you know that? Only man makes war out of sheer blood lust. He loves to kill. And only man has invented such weapons of destruction as would overcharge your little brain. A rain of fire."

A chill went through Cocky. It was as if he had forgotten her entirely and was speaking to himself. His eyes glowed. Was he crazy? She did not dare to move.

"Around the globe, find me a place at peace. Everyone quarreling, bickering, fighting. I feel as though I'm beating a brush fire with a broom and I no sooner stamp out the flames in one part of the forest than the fire spreads underground, under the pine needles, and springs up behind my back, and I'm surrounded by tongues of flame, and any one of them can ignite a nuclear warhead, and then good-bye to the whole kit and caboodle . . . and maybe good riddance too . . . We'd save the whales perhaps with our own deaths. Dear God, help me." He removed his glasses and rubbed his eyes between his thumb and forefinger.

After a moment he looked up at Cocky, and in his eyes she saw only raw suffering. "I shouldn't say that, should I? Do I frighten you with my vision of mankind? Well, don't worry. If I do my job well enough, perhaps you'll live to adulthood. You may have children of your own someday. I wonder if they'll be any better than the lot of mankind that walks the earth today. Oh, I know . . ." He waved his hand before his eyes, a futile, half-finished gesture. "I know. I shouldn't tell you man is bad."

Cocky said nothing. She tucked her feet under her on the chair and pulled Isabel half onto her lap. It occurred to her that the Secretary of State might be weeping.

"What's your name?" he asked suddenly.

"Cocky," she murmured, the words hardly audible. "Cocky Norton. It's short for Katharine Anne."

"Cocky Norton," he repeated. "Do you believe that man is bad?"

She said nothing.

"Go on, answer me," he insisted.

"I'm not old enough to know," she whispered. "I don't know about mankind. But I believe that individual people *try* to do good and then lots of times they don't manage to succeed."

He gave a laugh. "Another one for you. All right. Tell me, what would you do about the Middle East? Do you know anything about that?"

She shook her head.

"Well, that's what I'm doing sitting here in this tent, as you so politely pointed out, when I'm supposed to be over there making peace. I'm waiting for the President, you see, to come talk about the Middle East." He drew a breath. "It's a complicated story.

"More than thirty years ago, just after World War Two, the Jewish people were given a country of their own in an area called Palestine. I won't go into the reasons why, but it was our position, that of the United States, I mean, that the reasons for creating this nation were good and just."

He rose and began to pace the length of the tent. Cocky realized he wasn't talking to her at all, or rather that her presence served merely as the excuse for him to dissect the case. She listened attentively, one hand stroking Isabel.

"But in order to create this new country, the people who lived there before, the Palestinians, were moved out of their homes. They called it home. It was a desert. They were poor. No one listened to their side. That's how it is when you're poor. And they were Arabs. That's important too. The Arabs have a different religion, different customs, different language, and some are dedicated by holy vows to the destruction of Israel. Because Israel, the new state, took in only Jews and was governed by Jews according to Jewish laws . . ."

He turned to Cocky. "And ever since then, they've been at war. Call it war." He waved one hand idly. "It's hard to call it peace, this tension between Arab and Jew. Like those brush fires seething underground. Dear God, I'm so tired. And then we have a few months of uneasy truce, and the two sides withdraw for a time and wave their spears and shout across the gullies to each other and brag about what they'll do—only they aren't spears they wave but highly technical weaponry: missiles and mortars . . . Then every now and again they burst out in a fight and one side will rush in at night and tear up an enemy town, and the buildings crash down on the heads of the people living in them and refugees pour out, starving, begging, rummaging in the rubble for the dead bodies of their fathers and wives and children . . . And then that's a great victory, don't you see, and everyone rejoices at what was done. Only the next night the ones that were just attacked will retaliate. And *they* sneak into the enemy towns for a similar raid. And pretty soon they're at each other's throats . . .

"I'm making this sound very simple. It's not. Because there aren't only two sides to the dispute, Arab and Jew. No, there are a dozen factions in the fight; and anyone who joins a group (you'll discover this when you grow up), people who join such organizations believe passionately in their own ideas and tolerance does not exist. Some are Leftists, and some Rightists, and some believe in using violence. The worst are the international terrorists. They throw bombs, hijack airplanes, kidnap helpless people and hold them for ransom."

"But why?"

"To publicize their cause. To achieve their goals, that's why! And those committed to violence quarrel with those who don't use it, even when both want the same goals."

He threw himself back in his chair. "Oh, but even this description makes it sound too simple, because they don't even all agree on the goals. Oh, no. One group in Israel wants to make peace and others are afraid that if they give an inch they'll be driven from the face of the earth. Their families were killed, you see, in those holy wars ... Hate breeds hate. It's the same with the Arabs. Some are moderate but others refuse to admit that Israel even exists. On their maps you won't see Israel marked ...

"Oh, Cocky, God save us from people who feel passionately about anything! Now we're heading for another war. Perhaps a nuclear war this time. And if the United States or the United Nations cannot make peace—if I can't do it ... I know, I'm taking this personally. I shouldn't get so ... But they'll blow us all up in their war."

"Where do they get the weapons?" Cocky asked after a moment, at which he flinched.

"Oh, they buy them from us," he said bitterly. "Or from the Russians. Or the French, or the Germans. Weapons are easy to buy."

"And the people who had been living there?" she pursued. "I don't understand. What happened to them, when Israel was founded?"

He leaned forward, elbows on his knees. "They had no place to go, and so they lived—and their children have lived—" He laughed again, a brittle, humorless bark. "—in Utopia. Do you know the meaning of that word? It means 'no place.' Nowhere. Usually it's used to mean Paradise, isn't that odd? Utopia."

"But you can't take someone's home away and not expect him to be mad!"

"Of course not. It's perfectly understandable. The Palestinians were removed from their homes and have no country to call their own. Don't you see? *Both* sides are right. *Both* sides have claims to justice, and each has inflicted grievous harm on the other.

"Now Israel lives in a state of armed siege. Three million Jews surrounded by a hundred million Arabs. Every day they wake up thanking God they're still alive. It's a very small country, you see. Only it is also very warlike and ferocious. Four times the Arabs attacked Israel and four times that country captured Arab lands. Now the Arabs want their captured lands back, and the Israelis say if they give them back they'll be attacked again. Neither trusts the other. Both claim the land . . ."

He glowered at Cocky. "So tell me the solution to that one, if you can. There was a time when I had them sitting together at the same conference table. Peace, right in the palms of our hands. And now, thirty years of work, wiped out! God save us. I don't see what more we can do."

"No, you must keep them talking." Her words exploded in her mind, images, fragments; in her agitation she hardly knew what she was saying. "It doesn't matter if they disagree. Just keep them talking, keep them trying. It won't bring peace. Two people who hate each other can't help but fight, because even people who love each other fight; and if all these people want the same space and there isn't anyplace else for them to live, what can you expect? They can't possibly be asked to share. That's only the ideal. Sharing's just a *goal*," she said, the words tumbling from her lips; and whether she was talking about foreign policy or her mother and father or herself and Psi she could not have said, so confused were all three in her mind.

"But the *trying* is enough, because if they keep talking they won't break out in fights. So you can't let them give up. Just *to try* for peace keeps peace!"

She stopped and dropped her head on Isabel's to hide her emotion. What had possessed her to talk like that to this man?

The Secretary of State regarded her solemnly. "Oh, Cocky," he whispered. "Were you really sent to me by God?"

Chapter 11

The Secretary of State poured two glasses of iced tea from a silver pitcher and handed one to Cocky.

"I'm just discouraged, you understand." He sank back into his chair. Isabel crept to his side and lay down against his foot. Absently he scratched her ear. "You mustn't take what I say too much to heart. I'm just tired. So tired . . ." His voice trailed off. He closed his eyes again.

A moment later he had bolted to his feet. "It's all very well to say keep them talking, but how? Just when we thought we had a chance at peace, the enemy knows every move we make!" He shook his head fiercely.

"There we sat around the huge round conference table. It was wonderful. All the delegates from the Arab states entered in their flowing robes. From the opposite door came the Jewish delegates in Western dress, and with them were the military advisers in uniform with braid and ribbons and medals clinking on their chests. There were representatives from ten other countries. What a meeting!" His eyes sparkled. "The table was littered with papers and documents and an army of microphones at each place . . . translators and aides moving quietly about . . . And then we found—" He looked at Cocky with an anguished gaze. "—that the enemy knew every comma in our plans. It's as if they'd read them in advance. I can't understand it. That's why I'm here," he added, "when I'm supposed to be in Geneva. In a few minutes the President will be arriving. I wish I knew what I was going to say."

Cocky set down her glass. "Sir. Mr. Sti— Mr. Stins—" she stuttered.

"You can call me Mr. Secretary," he interrupted with a smile.

"I'm sorry. Mr. Secretary, a few weeks ago I saw something. You were just leaving on a trip, and I was coming down the block to get Isabel, and you were sitting in your limousine and there was this pile of suitcases on the sidewalk, and just then a man came hurrying down the block and he was carrying a briefcase just like one of the ones on the sidewalk, and when he got to your car, he tripped and fell over the bags and then—" She stopped.

"What?"

"He took one of the briefcases on the sidewalk and left his there."

"*What?*" The Secretary of State leaped to his feet.

"Yes. He exchanged his for one of yours."

"Are you serious? I don't believe it."

"His was put in the car with all the others, and then everyone got in and you drove off. That was when you were on your way to Egypt a few weeks ago."

"But we had all our bags when we arrived! Andrews— Cocky, what did he look like, this man?"

"He was short and fat," she said. "I saw him again once after that. He has a wart on his chin."

The Secretary of State grabbed her shoulder in a painful grip. "Listen, if you are making this up . . . Do you have any idea what you're saying?"

She hung her head. "That's why I didn't say anything before. I didn't know what to make of it. And maybe it isn't important—"

"No," he answered. "Perhaps it's not. But perhaps we've been betrayed. You don't remember what the case looked like, do you?"

"Not really. It was brown leather, not as big as some of the others."

The tent flap lifted. "He's on his way," said the Secret Service agent. "Another five minutes."

"Thank you. Oh, Buck." He called him back. "Do you remember a few weeks ago when we were getting ready to leave for Egypt? Did you see a man trip over the bags on the sidewalk that morning just before we left?"

"Yes, sir. I was up at the front door," he answered. "And a man did fall, but he was all right. He went right off again. Is anything wrong?"

"No, no. It's nothing."

"Are you all right, Mr. Secretary? You look so pale."

"I'm fine. I'll be all right."

The Secretary of State took two turns of the tent in silence, then stopped before Cocky, watching her under bristling black brows. She squirmed under his relentless gaze. When he spoke, his voice was severe.

"Well, Cocky Norton, you have seen me here, and we have to do something about that. Cocky, tell me truthfully, can you keep a secret? Or are you the sort of person who likes to talk about everything she knows?"

He studied her carefully as she considered her answer.

"I don't know," she said. "I do like to tell things. But sometimes I don't tell everything I know."

"Cocky, listen." He leaned forward, placing his elbows on his knees, hands clasped as if in prayer. "What I have told you affects the safety not only of the United States of America but of the entire world. No one must know that you came here today. Or that you have been inside this tent. Or that you saw me here. Do you understand?"

She nodded dumbly.

"You must not tell a soul."

She nodded again.

"I am not in Washington, do you understand? As far as the world is concerned, I am in Geneva today."

"Yes, sir," she breathed.

"If you tell anyone—your mother, your father, a friend—if you boast, if you accidentally drop the wrong word, you could put us all in danger. Certainly myself."

"You mean you could be killed?" She was incredulous.

"I could be killed. Perhaps more important, our negotiations for peace would fail. War would break out again. This time a nuclear war. I tell you, Cocky, if there were some way of holding you prisoner," he said grimly, "I'd do it. I'd clap you in jail in a second. For the next few weeks. But I can't do that. I have no choice but to trust you." His voice sank so low that she could barely hear him. "Please, Cocky, don't let me down."

"I won't tell anyone."

"Promise?"

"Cross my heart," she said seriously. "Spit on a Sunday." She held out her hand. Surprised, the Secretary of State hesitated, then took it in his.

"That's a solemn promise," he said firmly. "Now, Cocky, it's time for you to go. By the gate. I'll lock it after you. Okay, there's no one looking. Go now. Run."

He pushed Cocky toward the entrance, and in another moment she was racing across the garden, Isabel at her heels. She unbolted the gate, slipped through, and fled down the alley toward the street. Behind her she could hear Isabel's deep baying from the garden.

At the street she stopped. A long black limousine was pulling up at the Stinson house. The block was crawling with security agents—each man the image of the others in sunglasses and business suit—scanning the houses and shrubs, searching the street for enemies. Cocky stood stock-still, openly watching the car. The security men talked discreetly over their walkie-talkies.

"X-ray, convoy," said one, brushing past Cocky on the run.

The car pulled to a halt. An agent snapped open the back door and stood back respectfully.

From the car a figure emerged, moving fast. A hat was

jammed low over his eyes, and as he took the steps to the Stinson house two at a time, he shielded his face with a newspaper. But Cocky gasped with recognition: it was the President! The front door opened as if on signal. He disappeared inside.

Behind him the limousine purred away down the empty street. The Secret Service agents strolled casually up and down, trying to blend into the speckled shade of a sleepy residential district on a hot summer's day. Only Cocky, running in T-shirt and jeans, seemed an intrusion on the silent street.

Chapter 12

Cocky tied Isabel outside Neam's Market.

"Wait just a minute." She patted the top of the dog's head. "I'll be right back with something for you."

Cocky often went into Neam's to spend her earnings on a rawhide bone for Isabel or a dog biscuit.

Inside, the store was icy cold. She shivered as she hurried down the aisles, choosing a box of Animal Crackers for herself and People Crackers for Isabel. At the cashier she had to wait in line. She stared idly at the automated cash register, at the woman choosing cheeses at the deli counter, at the pile of groceries that the man ahead of her was charging to his account. Finally her turn came. She counted out the change. "I don't want a bag, thanks."

She walked through the sliding electric door—and froze.

Isabel was gone.

It took her a moment to register the fact. The basset was not tied to the bright blue leash. The leash was not tied to the iron ring.

"Isabel?" She looked up and down the street. It seemed impossible that the dog would have wandered off . . . and yet, she could have pulled her leash free, Cocky supposed, and nosed off after some enticing scent.

"Isabel?" Cocky broke into a trot. But at the next corner the street was empty too. No dog in sight. "Isabel!" she called. She was getting scared. "Here, girl. Here, Isabel!"

Her eyes surveyed the street, the bushes, the ledges and alleys between houses.

She stopped a passing man. "Did you see a basset hound just a minute ago? With a blue leash?"

"No. I haven't seen a dog."

Then she was running in the opposite direction, down toward Wisconsin Avenue. The market put its garbage out in the back of the store, behind the parking lot. Perhaps Isabel had broken free and followed her nose to food ... She rounded the corner, but still there was no sign of Isabel.

"Isabel! Here, girl. Here, girl." Cocky was frantic. Where could she have gone? She turned down Wisconsin Avenue, winding in and out of passers-by.

"Have you seen a loose dog?" she asked every now and again. "A basset hound, dragging a blue leash?" But no one had.

Twenty minutes passed. Forty. And still she had not found Isabel.

She raced to her own house. No Isabel. She left the two boxes of crackers there and plunged once again into the street. She was breathing hard. How could Isabel possibly get lost? Isabel hated to move. Why would she run away?

Six blocks. Ten. "Here, Isabel." Tears sprang to her eyes and her throat convulsed in a single sob. In her imagination she could see Isabel slipping the leash through the iron ring. Over and over in her mind she retied that knot as she ran through the streets of Georgetown, calling, calling. Over and over she tried to remember how she had tied it. And by the time she stopped again near Neam's, outside the large gardens of the Episcopal Home for the Elderly, shaking and out of breath, she could not remember even having tied the knot at all. Had she simply looped the leash through the ring? But she *always* tied it tight. Impossible for the dog to get free.

Yet she had. And Cocky imagined the leash being pulled slowly through the ring and Isabel setting forth, nose to the sidewalk, her strong wiry tail whipping over her tricolor back. She imagined the dog, her dog, moving toward the street. One paw would almost step on her ears as she studied the smells of the sidewalk, and the smell would take her to the street, and Isabel, who had no more sense than a baby about cars, would drop into the gutter and then begin to cross the street. Cocky cringed as she imagined the horn blasting at the hound, the car screeching to a stop, and then Isabel lying under the heavy black wheels, bloody and still, crushed by tons of steel. The driver would look around warily and then hurriedly lift the stiff little body into his car—a thump as his door closed, and who would ever know where Isabel was? Or whether she were alive or dead. A hit-and-run driver. Cocky had heard about that sort of thing, except in this case the driver would have stolen the dog as well.

With difficulty Cocky pulled herself over the top of the high spiked iron fence and dropped into the gardens of the Episcopal Home. She could not imagine how Isabel could squeeze between those bars, but perhaps . . .

"Isabel," she called. "Here, girl, come on. Please. Please, Isabel, come to me now." *Oh, God*, she prayed, *please give me back Isabel. Please don't let anything happen to her. Please, God. Please, God.*

She searched through the box bushes, climbing the hill to the big brick mansion.

"Hey, you!" It was a caretaker, shouting at her.

She veered toward him, breaking into a run.

"Please, sir." She could hardly speak. "Please, I've lost my dog. Have you seen a basset hound?"

"No, I haven't seen a dog."

"I lost her just awhile ago. Just a short time ago. She was outside Neam's. I thought maybe she squeezed through the fence."

"No, I haven't seen anything," said the caretaker. "Maybe it went home. Dogs do that sometimes."

"Go home?"

"Sure. Dogs are smart that way. They always know how to get home. Maybe she just got tired of waiting."

Cocky's heart gave a bound. "Yes." She turned and was racing down the hillside to the street, toward the Stinsons'. Perhaps Isabel had just gone home. *Please, God, please*, she repeated over and over, not even knowing anymore what she was saying or what she was praying for . . .

At the Stinsons' house she paused, looking up the steep flight of steps to the door. What if Isabel had not come home? Or what if she had come home and then they knew that Cocky had not taken proper care of her? Involuntarily she wrung her hands, turning away. The tears were trickling down her cheeks, her courage failing her. But again that image came to her of Isabel lying under the wheels of a car, bleeding in the road. She charged up the steps.

She rang the buzzer, jiggling in agitation. Never had the agents seemed so slow in answering. She yelled into the dead intercom. "Please, it's me, Cocky. Is Isabel there?"

The intercom crackled. "What is it?" The voice was puzzled.

"It's me. It's Cocky. I walk the dog."

The door opened.

"We can hear you, honey," said Charlotte. "Don't shout." She looked in surprise at Cocky. "Where's Isabel?"

Cocky stared wordlessly into Charlotte's eyes.

"Why, Cocky, honey, what is it?"

She leaned against the doorway, shaking with sobs. "Oh, Charlotte, she's gone. I've lost her. I can't find her."

"You what?" Charlotte stared down at her uncomprehending, then turned. "Miz Stinson," she yelled. "Miz Stinson!"

"I'm upstairs," called a gentle voice.

"Miz Stinson, you better come on down right now. Your dog's been gone and lost."

It was a brutal way to break the news.

A patter of feet on the carpeted stairs, and Mrs. Stinson, flustered, appeared at the door.

"Oh, Cocky," she said. "Come inside, dear." She put one arm around her. "What's happened? Now get control of yourself. Stop crying and tell me exactly what happened."

"Oh, Mrs. Stinson, I don't know what's happened. I was walking Isabel, and I tied her up outside of Neam's. I wanted to buy her a dog treat, and I tied her to that iron ring they have for dogs, and when I came out she wasn't there. She's wandered off, and I've looked and looked. I ran all the way to M Street and up as far as R, and I've asked people, and no one's seen her, and I can't find her anywhere." She looked hopelessly into Mrs. Stinson's eyes. "I thought maybe she'd come home."

"Oh, my goodness." Mrs. Stinson sank into a chair. "Oh, dear. What will John say?"

"Well, he ain't goin' to be happy 'bout that," said Charlotte. "How that man dotes on that dog!"

Her words were hardly designed to make Cocky feel better.

"Oh, Mrs. Stinson . . ." But somehow the words stuck in her throat. She couldn't speak for her sobs.

A man appeared in the doorway. "What's the problem?"

"Oh, Jerry, it's Isabel. She's lost. Cocky tied her up outside the market and the dog has wandered off."

He frowned thoughtfully. "Maybe she'll come home. Dogs do that."

"What do we tell the Secretary?"

"Uh-oh." Charlotte rolled her eyes to the ceiling.

"Now, look. She's wearing a name tag with her address," said the Secret Service agent. "She's just run off. Someone will return her."

"Is there anyone she knows?" Mrs. Stinson twisted her rings thoughtfully. "Someone she'd have gone off with?"

Cocky's thoughts flew to Psi. Had he taken Isabel as a joke?

"Can I use your phone?"

She dialed his number with shaking fingers. She danced from foot to foot. One ring. Two. She glanced around her. There was no sign that only two hours before, the President had visited this house, only two hours earlier she had sat in the garden tent with the Secretary of State. Four rings. Five. *Please answer, Psi . . . Dear God*, she prayed, *please make him answer the phone.* Eight rings. Nine.

Chapter 13

"**I**'ve got him." The roast-beef man pulled at Isabel's blue leash. "Come on, get out." She dug her paws deeper into the car seat.

A second man appeared at the window, regarding Isabel with interest, and she was hit by the horrible combination of stale cigars and hair oil.

"Come on, get out." The first man, the one who smelled of roast beef, pulled at Isabel's leash. "It's bigger than I thought," he said.

He was pulling on her collar now, until she thought she'd choke. "Come on, doggie," he crooned. "Nice doggie." Unable to breathe, she crept forward on the seat. She did not like it here. "Nice doggie." He dragged her forward until she was forced to jump to the cold cement. She sniffed at the odor of grease and oil, of metal tools and rubber tires.

"Come on, over here." The roast-beef man dragged her to a corner and tied her leash to a pipe. Tentatively, she wagged her tail. She was uncertain whether these men were friendly or not. Yet at first the one who smelled of meat had seemed so nice . . .

"How'd you get it?"

"It was tied up outside a market."

"Anyone see you?"

"No, but I thought that kid would never let it out of her sight."

"Okay. Let's go." The cigarman held the door for the roast-beef man to pass. From her corner, Isabel could see a garden and smell the fresh-clipped grass.

The door slammed shut behind them. Isabel was alone— and terrified. Until the very last moment she had kept on wagging her tail. They had not noticed. Now she bumped her bottom to the cold cement, sitting down to look about and catch her breath. It was all so strange. First the roast-beef man had come up to her while she was waiting for Cocky outside the market. Patiently she had permitted him to pat her. Strangers often patted her, and she had learned to be polite.

But this one was different. He gave her a slice of roast beef. It was delicious. She had licked it from his long knobby fingers gratefully and whipped her tail to show her pleasure in his gift. Not everyone thought to feed her roast beef.

"You want some more?" he had asked softly, untying her leash. "Come over to my car." He had glanced swiftly up the street, then, holding another slice of meat just out of reach, he had rushed her to the curb, opened the door of the waiting green Ford, and closed the door behind her.

On the floor lay a whole pile of roast beef on some waxed paper. By the time Isabel had finished it and looked up expectantly, ready to return to Cocky, the car was moving. She was surprised.

"You like to ride, doggie?" The man had talked to her all the time as he wound the car skillfully through traffic. He did not talk like the people she knew, her beloved master or Mrs. Stinson or Cocky. He had a harsh guttural voice and spoke with a foreign accent.

Isabel had pulled herself onto the car seat.

"Oh, you want to see out the window?" he had said. "That's all right with me. Look all you like."

Isabel liked cars. She liked the rocking under her body and the strange way that things had of suddenly whipping past the window: houses, trees, trucks. She had never figured out why these things began to move as soon as she got inside a car, but she enjoyed it all the same.

She was sure that in a moment the man would return her to Cocky; and then she would leap up on the little girl and lick her hands and face to let her smell the roast beef, and then the two of them would walk on home to dinner.

Isabel was astonished when they continued to drive. The smell of city streets was replaced by that of grass. A river rushed by with a thunderous watery roar, and this was followed by a blur of forest and woods. The air grew cool against her skin, and the earth twisted and turned, lifted up and dropped down for a long time. Finally they slowed and pulled into a driveway. A house crept up toward the car. It was made of stone and behind it came crawling a garage. The garage swallowed the car, which stopped. The roast-beef man got out. Another man's voice was heard, and the two talked for a while. Then the garage door closed with a squeal and Isabel was plunged into darkness.

It was then they pulled her from the car and tied her up. Now she sat in the dark. She was alone. She was scared.

Deep in her throat a whimper began. It turned into a cry that erupted in a sharp bark. The sound hit the ceiling like a stone and bounced back against her ears. It sounded good. She barked again—a single short rough note. Again the echo cracked against her ears. It made her feel less lonely.

She let loose a barrage of barks, and as the sounds soared to the rafters, surrounding her, enfolding her, the barking changed to that deep throaty baying that comes so naturally to any hound and is to them the most beautiful song of all.

She sat on her tail and howled.

She sang of fear and how awful it is to be alone in a dark, cold, strange garage; and as the sounds rose up around her she was pleased to think that the men would certainly hear and remember to come rescue her.

The door opened. It was the roast-beef man.

‏"اسكت يا كلب يا غبي"

Isabel looked at him in surprise. She did not understand Arabic.

As he approached her, she rose and whipped her tail politely. Now he would take her home.

On seeing her wrinkled anxious brow, he repeated his command in English. "So shut up! No more barking, hear?"

To her astonishment he turned to leave. The door had hardly closed when she howled again.

The man returned. He raised one arm. "If you don't shut up—"

She was silent, tail flapping gingerly against the cold cement.

Again he turned to leave. Again she bayed in misery.

This time he turned on her and kicked her in the ribs. *Ooooooh.* Now her howling rose to the heavens. Isabel had never been kicked in her life. She cried and cried.

"Hey, Sameer!" The cigarman had returned. He was shouting above her wails. "What's going on?"

"It won't be quiet."

"Well, we can't have him howling like that. The neighbors will be calling us in a minute."

"Shut your mouth!" Sameer kicked her again.

The cigarman grabbed Sameer. "You stupid ass. Don't you know anything about animals?" He patted Isabel's head with a smelly hand. "There, there. No more barking now, okay? I'll untie you and take you inside."

Isabel decided that maybe her first impression of this man had been wrong. He was short and squat and had a horrible smell, but he stroked her reassuringly as he bent to horrible smell, but he stroked her reassuringly as he bent to look at the tag on her collar. "Her name's Isabel," he announced to the roast-beef man. "It's a girl dog."

"Come on, doggie," said Sameer, ignoring the name.

They led her through the portico into a garden enclosed by a high stone wall. From there another door led into a kitchen with almost no smell of food and then to other rooms with no rugs or furniture. Isabel's nails clattered on the bare floors. She was in an empty house.

"Bring her to the lab. We may as well get started."

Down a steep flight of stairs to a basement. The walls sweated with moisture. Through another door and they were inside a spare white room, where white counters gleamed under hot white lights. It reminded Isabel of the vet's. She sniffed the bitter acid scent of disinfectant.

"Come on, doggie." Suddenly she was lifted bodily and placed inside a cage. Horrified, she braked with both front paws and turned around, scrabbling to get out; the door closed in her face. Where was she? She whined and pawed the bars.

"Is everything ready?" asked Sameer.

"It won't take long. It goes inside the collar. You won't be able to see it at all."

Sameer cracked his knuckles with a loud report.

"What are you doing now?"

"Still working on the trigger. Get me the collar."

The smell of roast beef filled her nose as Sameer opened the door of the cage. He held Isabel back with one strong hand against her chest while he unbuckled her collar with the other hand. Then the door closed on her again. Isabel felt naked without her collar. Now she was more confused than ever. With a whimper she circled around the cage and dropped down, her nose on her front paws, staring through the door in misery.

"She looks sad." Sameer cracked his knuckles again.

"She'll look sadder when she blows up," laughed the other. "Or blows up the Secretary of State."

"You want more meat?" Sameer approached the cage. "Here, doggie, just a scrap left in my pocket."

Daintily she licked the tiny offering from the tips of his long fingers, then lay back again. How odd that one moment he should kick her and the next give her food. She did not understand anything.

She rested her nose on her paws once more, and shut her eyes.

"Karl?"

"What."

"When will it go off?"

"About four in the morning. By then the dog will be back home and fast asleep in bed."

"What if he's not killed?"

"He will be. It's a powerful bomb. And according to our sources the dog always sleeps at the foot of his bed. Right on the blankets."

Nervously Sameer cracked his knuckles once again.

"I wouldn't sleep with a dog," laughed Karl. "All those fleas."

There was silence, except for the rush of air from a Bunsen burner, flaming on the counter. "Steady now. Steady." The air in the room was close. It made Isabel sleepy.

"Will you be glad when this is over, Karl?" asked Sameer. "I don't like it."

"Calm down."

"I'm an intellectual. I make reports. This business of bombs—"

"Are you scared?"

"Blowing up innocent—"

"Sameer!" It was a sharp command. "It is not your place to question the party."

"I'm not questioning."

"An international terrorist group lives by violence."

"I just don't like it."

"You're a fool. The Israelis steal Arab lands and now with this proposed peace plan they will keep them all. Just you wait and see. Anyway, our plans are set. It's too late to back out."

"I still don't like it."

"John Baron Stinson is the only man in the world who can bring this peace settlement to pass. It is our job to see he does not."

Sameer paced nervously from Isabel's cage to the counter where Karl was working on the bomb. "I wish I had a cigarette. You don't have a cigarette, do you?"

"Smoking's bad for you," Karl muttered. "Causes cancer."

Sameer snorted.

Karl looked up angrily. "What's the Secretary of State doing in Washington, anyway? He ought to be in Geneva. Serves him right if he gets blown up."

"It does?" Sameer was surprised.

"Only our revolutionary party knows that he is here. Our spy network is truly remarkable. When word gets out that he was killed in Washington—that he wasn't anywhere near Geneva—it will create panic. The peace settlement will collapse."

"I just wish it were over."

"You haven't any guts."

"Too many things can go wrong."

"Nothing can go wrong. Now be quiet. I'm making a bomb."

"I wish cigarettes weren't hazardous to your health," Sameer said wistfully.

Isabel was wakened when the cage door opened. "Here, doggie. Here's your collar." Then her leash was snapped to the collar and she was led back through the house and out to the garage.

"Now don't waste any time," snapped Karl.

"I won't."

"And for God's sake, just push her out of the car near the house and drive away. She'll walk home by herself. But get her onto her own block."

Sameer cracked his knuckles sharply. "I know."

"And don't let anyone see you."

"Hop in, doggie," said Sameer. "It's time for you to get to work."

Isabel looked up at him trustingly. Then she pulled herself into the car.

Chapter 14

Psi propped his back against a boulder. Below him the hillside plunged straight down in a wild tangle of fallen trees and brambles to the creek bed below. The area, remote and gloomy, matched his mood. From the distance he could hear the soft *swish-swish* of cars passing on the highway, a sound as lonely as the wind.

Psi reached into a brown paper bag and pulled out a pack of Marlboro cigarettes, followed by a pint bottle filled with dark brown liquid. He read the label aloud. "Jack Daniel's. Eighty proof."

Psi had never inhaled a whole cigarette before, much less tried a slug of whiskey. Now he tore the cellophane wrapping from the pack and threw it carelessly down the bank. He tapped out a cigarette against his fist in the sophisticated way that he had seen in the movies, and pulled the cigarette out of the pack with his teeth.

Many times he had seen his Pa do that, and follow the first drag with a shot of whiskey.

"*Whoooeeee!*" he'd say, and grin over at Psi and shake his head. "*Yeeeaaah!* Strong likker and weak women, that's the life for a man."

Psi lit the cigarette and inhaled deeply. Instantly he felt his lungs aflame. They crackled like black paper. He had not expected smoking to be hot. His throat tightened and tears smarted in his eyes. Slowly he blew out the smoke, watching it disappear in the soft summer air.

It tasted foul. He didn't care. He was going to act like a man. He took another drag. Then he unscrewed the cap from the whiskey bottle. After the first drink his father would grow surly. Then he slumped down on the shabby sofa and propped his feet on the scarred coffee table. "Look at you, scattering magazines all over the floor like that," Aunt Brenda complained. After a few drinks he would pick a fight.

Psi tipped the bottle to his mouth. The hot liquid hit his throat, his chest, and then his stomach and seemed to curl outward against his ribs. He was racked with coughs.

"Don' you look at me like that, boy," his father had said on that last visit to Psi's house. He had been drinking all afternoon. "Them eyes." He spat the words out at his son. "Jest like your mother. All so dainty-fied."

"No, I'm not," Psi had muttered unhappily.

"What? What's that you say?"

"I said I'm not dainty."

When his Pa got in these moods Psi was careful to stay out of his way.

Psi watched the smoke curl thin and blue from the cigarette in his hand. He took another drag. The scalding heat filled his lungs. He felt dizzy. He closed his eyes. The earth twisted under him. He felt sick. He stared at the small brown bottle in his hand, then resolutely took another swig.

After the fourth drink his father usually beat him, and so Psi had learned to leave the house whenever his Pa came home. Except for the last visit, when Psi had bounded into the house from soccer practice, tired and filthy. He'd pushed open the front door and stopped. His father was on the sofa, already well on the way to being drunk. His black eyes danced.

"Well, ain' you gonna say hello to yer Pa?"

"Hello." Psi had balanced at the door, wary, ready to bolt.

"Come here, boy. Don' you go way." His father's voice

was angry. "That ain' no way to greet yer Pa after a year you ain' seen him."

"Where's Aunt Brenda?"

"She's out. Come here." He beat the sofa cushion beside him with his fist.

Psi did not move.

"So it's *Aunt* Brenda now, is it? She ain' yer aunt."

"She's a cousin."

"Cousin!" his father had laughed. "She's so distant she don' hardly count for a relative. She's a foster mother. Takes you in fer pay from the Juvenile Board!" His eyes had glittered as he watched Psi's face. "Gettin' big, aincha? Come here."

Slowly Psi had moved into the room.

"Come on. I'll injun-wrestle you. See if yer big enough to beat yer Pa."

Psi groped unsteadily to his feet. The bank, the woods, were spinning. He wanted to laugh. He felt hot, filled with excitement. In one hand he held his lighted cigarette, in the other the bottle of whiskey. Suddenly he let out a yell. He swung the bottle around his head. He felt like dancing. He took another swig, then threw the half-empty bottle down the slope. It bounced from a tree, hit a rock, and shattered. A sluice of brown liquid rose in the air, hung suspended in the light for a full minute (or so it seemed to Psi), and splashed back down to earth.

He threw back his head and laughed, then crashed down the bank toward the broken bottle. The neck was still intact. He smashed it down against a rock, sending splinters of glass into the air. How they flashed! He howled with delight.

"Hey, you!"

Psi looked up. The policeman was seated on his horse. He looked gigantic against the sky. Psi felt as if his brain were floating away. He shook his head, and the movement caused him to lose his balance. He pitched forward and sprawled on the ground.

"Hey, what are you doing down there?"

"Doin'? I ain' doin' nothing." Psi's voice had the same high whine as his father's. He hated that voice. He hated his father. How strange to hear it in his mouth.

"Come up here," said the policeman. The horse danced to one side. "Don't you know any better than to smoke in the woods in this dry weather? You can start a fire."

"Don' you talk to me like that."

The policeman reined his horse around. He squinted at the boy with sudden recognition. "I know you. You started that riot outside the movie theater a few weeks ago."

"What if I did?" Psi stumbled up the bank.

"I warned you once, I warn you again. You better straighten out or you'll end up in jail."

"I ain' done nothin'. Don't give me any of that." Psi was pleased to hear the hard adult edge in his voice. Now he was acting like a man.

"Don't you sass me, boy."

Psi pushed past the horse angrily and stamped up the hillside. He held himself very straight, but he could not keep from weaving slightly to one side. He felt sick. His head was throbbing, and his stomach churned. He tossed the butt of the cigarette to the ground and squashed it casually with his foot, as if it were his own idea. Then he turned to look behind. The policeman was sitting on his horse, watching.

Psi pushed on until he was hidden by a turn in the path, then he broke into a run. Out in the meadow, he threw himself to the grass. The earth wheeled under him sickeningly.

He was filled with rage at the policeman. At himself. At the whole world. Everything he touched seemed to wither and die. His friendship with Cocky left him in turmoil. He hated himself for liking her. He hated himself for not being able to smoke a cigarette without turning green, for getting sick on a few swallows of liquor. He also hated himself for trying to get drunk. His father was a drunken bum who beat him; his mother had run away when he was four. Why? Was he so hateful that even his mother could not stand the sight of him?

Aunt Brenda cared for him only for the pay. Psi was swept by unbearable loneliness.

He lay on the grass for a long time. After a while he rose unsteadily. He had reached a decision. He would run away. It seemed clear that it was the only thing to do. There was no reason for him to stay in Washington. Aunt Brenda would not miss him. His father would be glad. Cocky did not care, and any dreams he might have had of school, even college . . . oh, these were foolishness. He was plunged into despair. He would pack a knapsack of clothes, some food, a book. He would hitchhike west. He'd leave today . . .

As Psi opened the door, the telephone was ringing. He started to reach for it, then changed his mind. No one wanted him.

Still it rang. Five times . . . six . . .

He moved to the kitchen.

Seven rings . . . eight . . .

At the tenth ring he raced to answer it. "Hello?"

There was a click, followed by silence. Whoever it was had hung up.

Chapter 15

Sameer slowed the car as traffic halted just beyond Key Bridge. He had forgotten the Saturday night crowds in Georgetown. Cars crawled up the street bumper to bumper, occasionally bursting out in raucous honking. Laughing couples gaily dressed and groups of threes and fours spilled across the sidewalk and wound in and out of the cars in the street as if they owned the streets as well. The music from a nearby car radio floated to Sameer in the night, mixed with the blaring rock-and-roll from a loudspeaker at a store. The lights from a hundred shop windows played on the street.

Isabel pulled herself up to peer out the open window and sniff the cool night air.

"Here, you're all tangled in your leash." Sameer unclipped the leash from her collar and unwound it from her paws and belly. She looked around at him gratefully, wrinkling her nose at the faint delicious odor of rare roast beef. She was hungry. She wished he would feed her.

A car horn blasted in her ear, an angry blare that was picked up and relayed from car to car like impatient elephants trumpeting in a herd. The street was filled with the honking of stalled cars. The cars strained forward in the milling crowds, the din of music, horns, voices, rose in the air.

Sameer leaned on his horn too. The cars did not move. He drummed his fingers on the steering wheel, glanced at his watch, shifted in his seat. "Come *on!*" He longed for a cigarette. He picked up the crumpled pack on the dashboard and searched inside with two fingers. Empty. He tossed it angrily to the floor and threw one arm against the door. *"Come on!"*

Traffic crawled forward half a car length and stopped again. Then Sameer spotted the newsstand. He opened the car door and peered at the line of cars ahead: it seemed endless. Nothing moved. Again he glanced at the newsstand, and at that moment his craving got the better of him and he decided to take the risk.

"Wait here," he said to Isabel. Then, leaving the motor running, he crossed the road and jogged clumsily up the sidewalk toward the stand. He was too heavy to run smoothly.

Isabel stared out the window. A great hollowness filled her. Now she was completely alone. And hungry. And lost. From somewhere nearby came the wonderful aroma of cooking meats. Her nose twitched. Her stomach growled. Then as the car horns rose again in thunderous clamor, the door to the restaurant opened, spilling forth a party of laughing men and women, together with a wave of smells that almost caused her to faint.

The next moment she had pushed through the open window, dropping heavily to the street. A stab of pain ran through her paws and shoulders. Then she ducked under the car and waddled up the street, winding in and out of the stalled cars as she followed the odor of food.

Sameer hurried back to the car. Now he saw that traffic had picked up and the cars ahead of his were moving, while those behind honked in wild delirium.

"Move it along!"

He threw himself into the driver's seat and released the brake. The car lurched forward a foot and stalled. The noise of horns enveloped him. He turned the ignition key and wrenched the car into gear with a screech.

It was only when he had lit his cigarette a few blocks farther down the road that he noticed Isabel was gone.

Chapter 16

Psi tossed some clothes in a backpack, wrapped a hunk of cheese and a cold chicken in foil, added two cans of Coke and then, having finished packing, he prowled the rooms restlessly. He was angry and bitter. But soon his mood changed. He began to think of Aunt Brenda, who had taken care of him for the last four years. True, she lit into him when he spilled things on her coffee table (which had been her mother's and which she treasured greatly) or spent his money on what she called "foolishness." But then she had so little money, and Psi, as she complained, was a constant trial: he skipped school or came home late or didn't turn up at the job she had found for him at the Safeway.

He looked one last time around this place where he had spent four years of his life. The living room was furnished with a sofa and the maple coffee table. A sagging easy chair in a faded pink slipcover stood near the fake fireplace. He leaned against the mantel, examining one last time the little china collection that Aunt Brenda prized. There were three blue china horses that galloped past a porcelain ballerina. There was a perky china cat, looking cutely out of the corners of its eyes. It towered over a collie dog, a shepherdess dressed in ruffles and bows, and her partner Little Boy Blue asleep. Psi thought they were horrible, but his aunt dusted each fragile piece lovingly. Out of fondness for her, Psi cared for them.

Now a great sadness welled up in him, and he thought

how she would worry if he just went off without a word. A minute later he threw himself down at the kitchen table with a pencil stub and the back of a marketing list.

He spent a long time on his note. When it was finished he propped it against the milkglass bowl above the sink. Then he dug in his pocket for his lucky rabbit's foot. Carefully he set it beside the letter. If anyone needed luck, he thought, it was his Aunt Brenda. As for himself, he still had a green rock with two white circles on it to protect him, and the tiny shell given him by Cocky.

"A cockleshell." She'd laughed up at him, showing him its delicate pinkish color. He looked around the room one last time, shouldered his pack, and left.

As the door closed behind him, he heard the telephone begin to ring again. He did not go back to answer it.

Cocky walked slowly down the block. "Here, Isabel," she called plaintively. "Here, Isabel." Her voice sounded flat and thin in the dark night. She was tired. Her feet burned. Her whole body ached. For almost five hours she had been walking the streets of Georgetown, searching for Isabel. Now it was ten o'clock at night, pitch-black, and she could hardly stand.

"Here, Isabel," she called; but her voice had lost all hope.

When Psi had not answered his phone earlier in the afternoon, Cocky had left the Stinsons' and, tired and discouraged, had made her way home.

By then her mother had returned from work. She was reading the newspaper, one stockinged foot tucked under her on the sofa, and a cup of coffee at her elbow.

"Oh, Mom!" Cocky threw herself in her mother's arms and burst into tears.

Her mother was astonished. She stroked her daughter's hair. "Cocky! What's the matter?"

"Oh, Mom! I've lost Isabel!"

It took Cocky a few minutes between her sobs to get the story out.

"... so I was hoping that she'd go on back home to the Stinsons', only she hasn't done that, and I've looked and looked everywhere!"

"Oh, darling." Her mother's eyes were wide with sympathy. "Maybe some family has found her and taken her in."

"But she has a name tag on," Cocky wailed. "Anyone would know who she belongs to. Oh, Mom, she's been stolen, I just know she has. And it's all my fault. And they've taken her off to sell to those laboratories that you read about where they do experiments on dogs with electric shock until they're dead. And Isabel—"

"Now stop that." Her mother took control. "You're letting your imagination run away with you. There's no evidence she's been stolen, and dogs get lost all the time. You've seen them yourself. And after a day or two someone picks them up and returns them to the owner."

"Oh, Mom."

"Now let me think."

"Please, Mom, can we go out in the car and look? I've been walking everywhere. Can you just drive me around to look?"

"Well, I have my self-awareness group at eight," her mother said tentatively. "But maybe. It's early yet. All right, I'll drive you around for a while. We'll knock on people's doors if you want. Did you notify the police?"

"Yes. And the Secret Service."

"I'm sure we'll find her," her mother said. She took a gulp of cold coffee. "Have you had anything to eat?"

"I'm not hungry."

"You have to eat something. To keep your strength up. You look awful." She ruffled Cocky's hair affectionately. "Now go wash up and lie down on the sofa for five minutes. I'll fix you something quick."

"A sandwich," Cocky said. "To take with us in the car."

"No, some scrambled eggs. You can just take ten minutes and eat properly."

The eggs, milk, and toast were almost the only food Cocky had eaten that day. After the first bite, she bolted them down. Then she and her mother drove slowly around Georgetown for an hour, looking for Isabel.

They also stopped at Psi's. Aunt Brenda answered the door.

"Is Psi here?" Cocky asked.

"Well, couldn't rightly say." She was dressed in a cotton housedress, and beads of sweat covered her expansive brow. She fanned herself. "It's so hot." In the cleft of her bosom Cocky could see a gold necklace with a charm inscribed "Life, Love, Laughter."

"What do you mean, you couldn't say?" Mrs. Norton asked.

"Well, he's *usually* home by now, and tonight he ain'." Her voice had a plaintive whine. "Only I don' know where he'd be. Do you?"

"If we knew we wouldn't be here to ask," Cocky laughed. She thought Aunt Brenda wasn't too bright.

"Oh, I guess that's so. Well, I sure hope he ain' been hurt. I brought his favorite dinner home tonight—pizza from that pizza parlor. You know the one? They cost more'n three dollars each. And then he warn't here." Her voice trailed off. "Now it's cold."

There was a pause. Cocky smiled at her.

"You'da thought he'd left me a note."

"Well, thank you anyway." Mrs. Norton looked away. "Tell him we were looking for him, please."

"If I ever see him again." She paused ominously.

Cocky exchanged a glance with her mother. "What do you mean?" asked Mrs. Norton.

"I'm jes worried sick. I cain' think where'd he'd a gone off to. Less'n he's been hit by a car."

"God forbid."

"Or been stole mebbe. I've heard they's people out, like to steal young kids."

"Well, Psi's not so young."

"No, but he's a nice-lookin' boy. They's lots a people might want to steal a boy like him."

A tear splashed down her cheek and along the fold of her double chin. She turned from the door and settled onto the couch.

"Oh, Mrs. Harvey." Cocky's mother sank beside her in sympathy. "Now don't you worry. I know he'll be back. When did you miss him?"

"Jes tonight. Jes when he warn't home tonight. Never come home for dinner. So I'm jes settin' here watchin' TV and waitin' fer the police to call. I figure they'll get to me sooner or later with the news."

"Now that's no way to talk," said Cocky's mother.

"Or mebbe it's his *father*"—she said the word as if it were a spider on her tongue—"come and took him off. He'd do that, if he's outa jail. I turned him in to the agency onct—"

"The agency?"

"Protective Services. What takes care of Psi and me. Ony they said we'd need a lawyer and go to court and all, and I somehow couldn't see that since the boy's Pa was across state lines again. And see what it gets you? Now he's done come and stole his son back and I won't never see him no more. He like to kill the boy someday. Then he'll go back to jail, I guess. Ony it'll be too late." The tears dropped crystal-clear off her chin to the soft swell of her breast.

Mrs. Norton was looking at her, jaw agape. "In jail!" she cried. "Good Lord, Psi's father's been in jail?"

"Well, when we're lucky. Ony he probly ain' there now, if he's done took off the boy."

"Now, Mrs. Harvey, you don't *know* that," Cocky's mother insisted.

"Well, but they's signs," said Aunt Brenda. "Lookee here, what I found. His rabbit's foot!" She held it up triumphantly. "Ain' nothin' he liked better'n his rabbit's foot. He'd never be without it. And it's jes a sign, I say, that he's gone and got in trouble."

102

"Where did you find it?"

"In the kitchen." She nodded vigorously as if in confirmation of the fact. "Propped up on a piece of paper with a lot of magical pictures on it. Jes *signs*, if'n you ask me."

"Can I see it?" asked Cocky.

"It's there in the kitchen. I wouldn't touch it. I tried to figure it out, but it's too much fer me . . . And now he's been stole—" She looked up at Cocky's mother, and her face puckered. The next moment she gave in to the full flood of tears.

Meanwhile Cocky had run into the kitchen and found the note.

"It's from Psi," she said, carrying it into the living room. "It's not magic. It's just a note."

"And why would he leave me a note without words?" Aunt Brenda turned on her indignantly. "He knows I kin read."

"What's it say?" Mrs. Norton peered over Cocky's shoulder at the note. It looked like this:

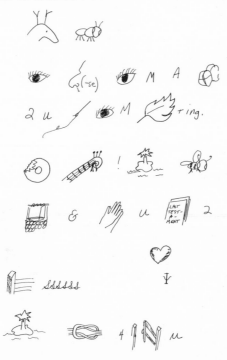

"Can you read that?"

Cocky slowly translated the message out loud: " 'Dear Aunt: I know I am a burden 2 you, so I am leafing. Donut fret!' Look at that! A guitar fret! 'Isle be well and pray u will 2. Love, Psi. Postscript: I'll not 4 gate you.' "

"Well, ain' that the oddest thing!" Aunt Brenda took the note. "Where does it say all that?"

Cocky explained the code, at which Aunt Brenda beamed with pride.

"And that little mark means psi!" she exclaimed. "I never seen the like of that boy for cleverness. Who'da thought he could say all that without words? He is the smartest boy!"

"So, he's run away," Cocky's mother said. The words seemed to snap Aunt Brenda back to tears.

"Run away!" She clutched Mrs. Norton. "Oh, I knew it'd be trouble soon's I come home and saw he warn't here. Oh, Lord God above, no tellin' what'll happen now. He'll be stole fer sure."

It took Cocky and her mother a while to calm her down. Finally they made her lie on the sofa, turned on the TV for company, and promised to call if they found Psi.

By then it was time for Cocky's mother to leave for her meeting. First she called the police to report the runaway. Then she dropped Cocky off at the house.

"Now we've got a lost boy *and* a lost dog! For heaven's sake, don't you go get lost."

"Oh, Mother."

"Honey," she said as Cocky opened the car door, "you don't think Psi could have gone off with Isabel, do you?"

Cocky shook her head. "No. He wouldn't do that. Oh, what am I to do? It's my fault Isabel is missing!"

"Oh, honey, I'd do anything to get out of this meeting tonight, but I can't. Call the Stinsons and see if Isabel has come home yet. If she hasn't, we'll look some more in the morning. Okay?"

"And we'll put some signs up on the trees."

Cocky was sunk in despair. With a heavy heart she kissed her mother good-bye.

"Now be careful. And lock the door behind you," her mother called after her.

The house seemed empty when Cocky entered. She telephoned the Stinsons, only to learn that Isabel had not yet returned. Then she wandered the rooms restlessly, turned on the TV, turned it off, looked in the refrigerator and slammed the door shut. It was a little after eight o'clock. In her imagination she saw Isabel hooked by her leash on a tree branch and slowly strangling to death; Isabel tired and thirsty and lost, hunting vainly for her home; Isabel locked in some stranger's house, desperate to escape.

Finally she could stand her thoughts no longer. She bolted from the house in search of her dog.

"Isabel," she called. "Here, Isabel." Sometimes she whistled: *Weeeeooooooooo.* But no answer came. For two hours she walked the brick sidewalks, calling, calling. Her feet hurt. Her legs ached. She was blocks from home.

She wished that Psi were with her. She leaned against the brick wall that ran along the street, and suddenly she felt so tired she began to shake. How many miles had she walked that day? A profusion of vines and shrubbery tumbled down the wall beside her. She could smell the rich sweet scent of honeysuckle. In the distance came the low rumble of traffic, the city sounds that never stop.

She traced the rough brick wall with her fingertips. It reached higher than her head. She walked along it until she came to the steps that led to the mansion and gardens above. She stared up the steps at the dark, empty house.

"Here, Isabel," she called faintly. She felt her way up the dark steps. "Here, Isabel." Her voice quavered—hardly more than a whisper in the summer blackness. At the top of the steps she turned to the side and crawled under the shrubbery that grew along the wall. Now she was above the street. She squirmed forward. The branches formed an arch above her head. The earth was a hard, cool clay; and there, hidden in her bower, Cocky closed her eyes, after hours of frantic searching, and in an instant was asleep.

When Cocky woke she could not imagine where she was. Cold and stiff from sleep, she lay on the hard earth blinking at the shrubbery. Whatever was she doing here? Then the loss of Isabel hit her like a rock. Slowly she backed out of the shrubbery. It must be past midnight, she thought, glancing at the rising moon. Her mother would be worried. She groped down the dark steps to the street, and—

"You fool!" The voice sounded almost in her ear. She pulled up short. "How *could* you lose the dog?"

For a moment she thought the words referred to her. Then she saw almost beside her the man who had taken Stinson's briefcase! Her heart lunged so hard it hurt.

"It wasn't my fault," said another voice. She shrank into the shadow of the steps and climbed them backwards, one foot after another, until, trembling, she sank into the protection of the bushes. From here she was above the street and higher than the men below.

"It wasn't my fault," the first voice mimicked angrily. "Then whose was it?"

Ever so slightly Cocky lifted her head to peer down at the sidewalk below. The short fat man was confronting a taller horse-faced man. Silently she dropped her head. She hardly dared to breathe, and though she did not know why she cared, she prayed they had not seen her.

"Karl, listen—"

"Shut up! You've done enough. How *could* you lose it?" The voice was a dry whisper, harsh as winter leaves.

"I told you, the dog jumped out of the car and ran away. I was caught in traffic, I tell you. How could I follow it?" Cocky lay rigid. Was it possible they meant Isabel? She forced herself to lie still, and now began the worst ordeal of her life,

for an ant was crawling up her arm. She could feel each leg
tickling as it crept forward, and she did not dare to move. She
could not brush it off. She forced herself to lie still. Suddenly
she felt another ant crawling up her thigh, and then a third,
and in torment the thought came to her that she was lying on
an ant hill. One itch after another flared up like spitfire on her
legs, her ribs, her nose. She itched all over. An army of insects
seemed to be crawling inside her shorts, along her back. She
sucked in air in long slow gasps, telling herself the ants were
only twitching nerves. Her heart was pounding so hard that
she felt the two men must surely hear it.

"What a mess you've made. Now we have a basset hound
running loose with a bomb in her collar."

Cocky's heart stopped with a thump. The ants all disappeared.

"Karl, it doesn't matter," whispered the voice of the
shorter man, and Cocky heard his knuckles crack so sharply
she jumped.

"Doesn't matter! Good God, Sameer, and they say you're
an intellectual! Listen," Karl hissed, "that bomb is set to go
off at four o'clock this morning. It is supposed to kill the
Secretary of State. Or had you forgotten that?"

"But it won't matter," came the miserable answer.
"When the bomb goes off, the dog will be destroyed. It's very
powerful. There won't be so much as a teaspoon of dog left for
anyone to find. No one can trace it back to us."

"You stupid ass," he hissed. "No one cares about the
dog."

Cocky could hardly believe her ears.

"The important thing is that it arrive home in time to
blow up the Secretary of State, can you get that through your
skull? That man must not return to Geneva, do you understand? We can't let him settle that peace agreement."

"So what are we . . .?" The rest was lost in mumbling.
The two men were moving off, and as anxious as Cocky had

been before that they should go away, she was suddenly equally aghast at their departure. Cautiously, she raised her head to look.

"We must find that dog!"

"Well, she jumped out of the car just on M street here. A block away," said Sameer. "We'd crossed the bridge. I'd stopped for a red light . . ."

Cocky could hear no more. In the dim glow of a far-off street lamp she saw them turn the corner, heading down toward M Street.

Cocky backed quickly out of the shrubbery and groped down the steps to the street. Her teeth were chattering. She was shaking so hard she could barely stand. For a moment she leaned against the cold, rough stone wall to support herself, then turned and raced in the opposite direction from the men. All she wanted was to be safely home.

Chapter 17

The first ride came almost at once. Psi had just reached the Virginia side of the river when the car pulled over: a Mercury Marquis.

"You need a lift?"

Psi liked the man's big beefy look, and he liked the solid white exterior of the vehicle and the creamy plastic seats. "Sure." He took it as a good omen that the car had stopped before he'd even lifted his thumb.

"Where to?"

Psi settled in the front seat. "I'm going—" He stopped. In fact he hadn't thought out clearly where he was going.

"How 'bout Richmond?" asked the man, with a chuckle of laughter. "Cuz that's where I'm heading, if that's all right with you." He had a strong Southern accent.

"Sure. Fine."

"You want a little music? Push in that tape deck for bluegrass. Or choose jazz, blues, bands, rock. Do you like music?"

"Hey, yeah." Psi pushed the tape into the cartridge and the air was filled with plucking banjos. "You really got it made." He glanced at the man admiringly. He could just imagine himself crossing the country in style.

"My name's Stu."

"Psi Ilyich." He was startled then by Stu's sideways leer.

"You been waiting long?"

Psi shook his head. They were on the highway now, heading south.

"I don't guess so. Nice-looking boy, that's why," said Stu.

Psi froze. What did that mean?

"Lots of times you can wait a long time," Stu continued. "But a nice-looking kid—boy *or* girl—they'll be picked up right away."

Psi said nothing.

They rode in silence for a time. Psi tapped his foot gently to the beat of the country music.

"You looking for some action?" Stu asked suddenly.

"Um." Psi was wary. "What do you mean?"

"Action. Fun."

"Sure," said Psi. "I guess."

"Well, maybe we can work something out." Stu grinned over at him. "Now me, I'm a salesman. Travel a lot. I have this whole area. Crystal City south. It's not bad. I'm in air conditioning. But a man gets lonely at times, you know what I mean?"

Psi's hand crept to the door handle. "No," he said.

Stu grinned at him. "Sure you do." He reached across the seat between them and rested one hand lightly on Psi's leg. Psi watched in horror. He could not move. The sandy, freckled paw against the blue of his jeans. The short, stubby fingers. Stu's hand squeezed his thigh ever so gently, the barest pressure, and returned to the steering wheel. Psi's forehead broke out in sweat. Suddenly the white imitation-leather seats in the gleaming white car, the windows sealed for the air conditioning, were stifling him.

"You're a nice-looking kid," Stu continued. "You could make a lot of money in the right business."

"I gotta get out." Psi blurted out the words. "Lemme out."

"What d'ya mean, you gotta get out?"

"I'm sorry. I forgot something. I— I'm not— I wanta get out."

110

Instantly the man pulled the car over to the shoulder of the road and reached angrily across Psi to open the door for him. "Go on, get out." He spat out the words. "You're all so high and mighty."

Psi scrambled out of the car, pulling his pack and skateboard after him. His knees were weak.

"I've met your type before," Stu shouted.

The next minute the car had roared away, and Psi was left on the road, consumed with fear and rage. "That kook," he muttered to himself. "That dirty kook."

After a moment he shouldered his backpack. It was eight o'clock at night, and all around him lay a tangle of superhighways looping in and out, a concrete pretzel on which moved a million cars. They streamed past, their headlights gleaming on the white cement road. As they passed him, the backwash of wind lifted Psi's shirt and flapped it against his back.

He counted cars: Pintos, Mustangs, Cougars, Rabbits, Impalas; Cordobas, Monacos, Coupes de Villes . . .

For a long time he walked along the edge of the road. He was chilly and tired. He stuck out his thumb. And now it seemed that simply wanting a ride was enough to ensure that no car stopped. Chevys, Pontiacs, Volvos, Mercedes, Cadillacs, Buicks, Lincolns, Fords . . . Another hour passed, and full night fell.

After a long time a battered pickup truck braked to a stop. It hit the shoulder just beyond him, raising a cloud of choking dust. Psi ran forward into the dust to meet it. He yanked open the door—and almost changed his mind.

The farmer wore a sweat-stained shirt and muddy boots. He was an old man, and when he turned his head Psi was horrified to see a livid blue-red birthmark smeared across his cheek.

"Where you going?"

Psi blinked in surprise, then threw his pack inside. The seat, made of coarse black cloth, was ripped in several places and mended with black tape, which had ripped in turn, letting straw and cotton stuffing spill out on the floor.

"Anywhere." He closed the door angrily.

"Well, I ain't going too far. Jes up toward Springfield way. But I reckon I kin take you a mile or two." He had to shout to be heard over the rusty motor. The muffler was broken.

"I'd be obliged." Psi stared out the window. He did not want to talk. He thought the man was dumb.

They rode in silence for a few minutes, then the old man leaned over toward Psi, shouting, "You look like my sister's child. I was about to pass you by, and then I saw you looked like my sister's child, thet's my nevew."

Psi bounced on the hard seat as the pickup rocketed down the highway.

"And I said, thet looks jes like Gene Kelsey. That's his name. But knew you warn't him cuz he's over towrard Leesberg way now. Goes to the new high school there. They moved down there a year or two ago now."

"That so?" Psi stared intently out the window. It seemed extraordinary how the old man wouldn't take a hint. The more silent Psi became, the more the farmer talked. Psi couldn't figure it out. He decided not to listen, he had no interest in the man. But no sooner had he made that decision than his mind flipped with full attention to the farmer—as if it were a machine over which he had no control. He wrenched his thoughts away and stared out the window. But his ears strained for the old man's voice. He hunched down on the seat, furious with himself.

"I don't hardly see 'em no more," the old man was saying. "I miss 'em too. That's my favorite sister, Sis. That's what we alays call her. Sis. I alays liked her best of all. They was nine of us, but I alays liked her best."

Psi said nothing. From the window he could see only the blurred pale reflection of his own face. He was annoyed at the old man for being stupid; and he was more annoyed at himself for listening to the stupid man. If he had any sense he'd know Psi didn't want to talk. But the man kept running right along as if Psi were politely answering.

112

"Y'know it's funny, seems like some people you like and you'll alays like 'em and ever'thing about 'em too. And other people you jes cain't abide."

He spat out the window. Psi sank deeper in the seat. If there was anything he hated, it was people who spit. His father liked to spit. He'd hawk up a glob of white mucus and land it on the sidewalk *splat* at your feet, or he'd hook one thumb in his belt and spit over his shoulder in a casual way. Then he'd look at Psi and laugh.

"That yer skateboard?" asked the old man in a friendly way.

"Yeah."

"Bet you're good, eh?"

"I'm okay." Psi was barely polite.

"I saw some kids on them things over in the Springfield parking lot. Boy, it was purty! I'd been fifty years younger, I'd a like to tried it myself." He chuckled happily.

A few drops of rain splattered the window.

"Rain," said the old man. "But 'twon't be much. Jes a sprinkle. Is it hard?"

"What?"

"The skateboard."

"No, but it takes practice. You gotta use your whole body. It's done by shifting your weight."

"You ever have an accident on one of them?"

Psi shook his head. "Nothing serious," he answered, and to his surprise he found himself chatting on and falling into the same country speech as the old man's. "But I've heard of people," he said. "A boy once over at Gaithersburg fell and busted his head open and broke a leg."

"I guess you been up to Washington for a good time, eh? You goin' home now?"

"Yeah," he said warily.

"Where you goin'?"

"Me?"

"Ain't no one else in this cab," the old man laughed. "Jes you'n me."

"Oh, down toward Richmond a way," Psi said. He hoped that would be vague enough.

"That where yer fambily's from?"

"Yeah." Psi figured if the man came from Springfield, he wouldn't know too much about Richmond.

To his horror the farmer continued, "Whereabouts? I know that area real well."

"Oh, just outside the city." Psi searched his memory frantically for a place name. "We haven't been there long. Just moved there."

"Over to the west? Near Goochland?"

"No-o," said Psi hesitantly. He was afraid the old man might know that area and trap him. He stared intently out the window. "Raining harder," he said, to change the conversation.

But the old man wouldn't take the hint. "Mebbe to the south of Richmond? They's some nice country down yonder. You-all from that part?"

"Why?" Psi turned on him. "Are you from there?"

"No," he laughed. "I'm from right up roun' here. Lived here all my life, 'cept when I was in the Army in the war. That's World War Two. Stationed in Texas then. And France. Now that's a purty country too. But I tell you, they ain' no place like the place whar you growed up. It's like yer own people, you know? Ain' none better."

Psi said nothing. He was disgusted with himself. He would have liked to close his ears and quit listening. Instead he was glued to the old man's words.

"I tell you somethin'. I think the whole world's gone crazy," the old man shouted above the motor. "Like everyone wants what he ain't got and he don't want what he has got. Ever'body wants a divorce if they're married. An' no one can stand to be with the same person or stay in the same place for more'n a year or two. But they're always roamin' here and there, gettin' in trouble." He spat out the window again. "And you know why? Cuz they don't care for nothin' in this whole wide world. Things get hard on 'em, or jes so they think they're bored, and the first thing you know, their feets are itchin' to move out. They never think to stick it out. And you know what?" He leaned toward Psi. "Time comes when they discover they're all alone in this world, and mighty lonely it is too. Yes, sirree. But it's their own fault they're alone, I say."

Psi said nothing. It was raining harder now. Large fat drops spattered on the windshield. The old man turned on the wipers.

"Then they go on dope and likker and the good Lord knows what all, and they raise hell, and turn to crime and land in jail. And why? I ast you." He paused, glancing over for an answer.

"Why?" Psi finally broke the silence.

"Cuz they're all alone!" he finished triumphantly. "An' there ain' a thing in all the world they cares about, seein' as how they're alays movin' from place to place, so fast they can't even get attached noways. And they ain' a person in the world to care for 'em, cuz they walk out on ever'body." He lifted his voice angrily. "No commitment. Times get hard— bingo! off they walks. People are soft. I seen times, I tell yer, when the crops are ruined by drought or bugs—or thet hurricane thet come through here a few years ago. Remember thet? River flooded my entire land. Right up to the cellar steps. I lost more'n a hunnert foot of riverfront. Mebbe an acre all told. My son says, 'Pa, why'n you sell out and leave? Thet ain' no way to make a livin', scratchin' at the earth. You don't make a dime.'

" 'Boy,' I said to him, 'I was born here and I'm fixin' to die right here on my own place. There's more to life than makin' a dime.' Hmph."

They drove in silence for a while. Psi bounced on the hard seat, wondering if all his rides would be crazies.

"Go?" shouted the old man. "And what do I have then, eh?" He turned to Psi angrily. "Nothin'! that's what! Nothin'. Stevie, he's my boy, he says, 'Sell, and you kin go ennywhere.

Move to Florida.' And what would I do in Florida? All my friends is here. My fambily dead in the cemetery right on my own land. You listen to me, boy, don't you *ever* lose sight of the people you love, you hear me?"

He pulled to a stop so suddenly that Psi smashed forward into the dashboard.

"Oh. You okay?" the old man shouted at him.

Psi fumbled for his pack. "I'm all right, thanks," he said. "I was just surprised." He reached for the door handle. His eyes caught the old man's sharp quick glance. He felt pulled by conflicting emotions. "Thanks," he said again.

"Hey, wait." The old man plucked his sleeve. "Here," he said. "You got any money?"

"Money?" Psi was taken aback.

"Hell, boy, I can tell you're runnin' away. Here, take this. You may need it." He stuffed some bills into Psi's jacket pocket.

"No, I can't take that."

"Now you jes listen to me." He spat out the open window again. "It's gettin' late out. Rainin' some. You got a long way to go to get to Richmond and I know damn well you ain' stoppin' there, and probly you ain' never been there neither. So you take thet. You'll need it."

"I—"

"Buy yerself a cup of coffee. Or a bed. Think of me. Thet'd give me pleasure, if you would." He said it so gently that Psi was truly touched.

"Thank you," he said simply.

" 'Nuther thing. Don' you take no lifts from nobody whose looks you don' like, you hear me? I mean thet now. They's a lot of rotten crazy folks out there thet'd think nuthin' of rollin' a kid for his money. Mebbe bash his head open with a wrench . . ."

Psi felt a wave of hopelessness at following that advice.

"Here now," said the old man. "Don't fergit your skateboard."

"Thank you." Psi was standing on the shoulder of the road, one hand on the open door. The man rubbed a stumpy finger across his birthmark.

"You don't owe me no thanks," he said. "You look so much like my sister's boy. I'd hate to think of him out here—" He turned his head away.

"You ought to go see her," Psi said. "She's not that far away. You should drive over—"

The old man shook his head. "Oh, hell." His eyes were a million miles away. "I cain't do thet, boy. She's dead. Died five years ago." He looked over at Psi. His eyes were miserable. "I jes tell myself she's still there, cuz it don't seem so hard to take. But I won' never see her no more till the good Lord takes me off too ... First it were my wife died. We'd been together thirty-five years. And the same month my sister—" He shook himself like a dog and turned fiercely to Psi. "That's why I tell you all thet, boy," he shouted. "Cuz we don' never know what people mean to us till they're gone. And when you finish in this life, why it's one or two people, that's all, thet you'll have to remember. Jes one or two people, or a good dog or a horse. Mebbe a couple good moments of yer life." He hit the steering wheel with his fist to emphasize his point. "And thet's the whole of it."

He stopped. Psi was looking at him in open-mouthed astonishment.

The old man grinned. "Never you no mind. Good luck to you, you hear. Good luck, and God bless you, boy."

Psi shut the door. The next moment he was alone in the darkness, the light rain slashing his eyes as he watched the red taillights of the pickup disappear up the exit ramp.

It was dark. His footsteps crunched on the gravel. No cars had passed for twenty minutes, and the last two had whipped by, drenching him in the spray from their tires.

Ahead the headlights lanced the road. He stuck out his thumb and stood farther into the highway. For a moment he was caught, spotlighted by the beams. The car hesitated, tore past, then squealed to a stop up ahead. It backed toward him, and suddenly he was waving it furiously away.

A woman stuck her head out the passenger door. "You want a lift?"

"No!" he yelled. "No, I don't." And he was sprinting across the slick highway toward the green median. His feet sank into the moist grass, and then he was over that and dashing across the far side. It was already late, but with luck he'd be back in Washington by midnight. His fingers curled around the cockleshell in his pocket. His heart sang. Now he had another plan. He couldn't wait.

Chapter 18

As Cocky neared her house she saw the figure crouched in the darkness under her bedroom window. Her blood ran cold. Now they were after her as well! She shrank into the shadows like a ghost and watched in horror as the figure stooped, one arm sweeping the earth at his feet. Evidently he found what he was looking for, because the next moment he straightened and threw up his arm toward her window.

Ping! She heard it strike against the glass. At that moment he turned toward the light—

"Psi!"

He whirled to face her.

She almost collapsed with relief.

"Cocky!" In a flash he was beside her, his arms hugging her. "I didn't want to wake up your mother," he said.

"I've been looking ev—"

"Cocky, I came back to get you," he interrupted.

"Get me?"

"I'm so glad to see you. Listen, Cocky, I'm running away, and I've come back for you. We have to go together, we belong together." He stopped at her startled look. "Please?" he said softly, and no one will know what that word cost him.

She stared blankly back at him. "Oh."

His arms were still around her, and he bent forward then and kissed her on the mouth.

Cocky had always heard that her first kiss—and by a boy

she liked—would be a dizzying experience. In fact it was not.

Psi had never kissed a girl before, and he pressed his mouth hard against Cocky's for a few seconds. His eyes were closed tight, like the hero's in a movie.

But hers shot open! His nose was right up next to hers. She felt more startled than anything else, and then—annoyed. It was like being kissed by the back of your hand.

Psi however, was more romantic. He pulled away, dazed. "You're the first girl I've ever kissed," he murmured huskily.

Cocky almost burst out laughing. She started to say "I know," but one look at Psi's face made her swallow the words. She ducked her head to hide her smile, and Psi's heart was filled with tenderness.

"Um," said Cocky. Luckily she was saved the necessity of any further answer, because Psi kissed her again, this time more gently; and this time, standing in the middle of the midnight street, she was overwhelmed by a rush of emotions: surprise, pleasure, tenderness, pride, gratitude, and then guilt at enjoying his kiss; and all these emotions tumbled through her higgledy-piggledy, until one, like a bubble floating softly upward from the black still waters of a pond—one finally broke to the surface and burst: it was her sense of the ridiculous. The idea of Cocky Norton in her dirty shorts and sneakers being kissed in the silent street in the middle of the night struck her as so funny she burst out laughing and pulled away.

She wiped her mouth with the back of one hand, then, seeing Psi's expression, laughed again, at her own rudeness. "Oh, wow," she said.

That made Psi feel better. "Run away with me," he pleaded. "We'll go out West."

"Psi, I don't want to run away." She grabbed his hand and plunked down on the front steps. "And anyway, we don't have time to run away. The whole world's about to explode practically, this very night, I've just discovered, and we've been looking everywhere for you. There's no time at all, and we've got to stop it."

"Stop what?" Her words and especially the urgency of her tone made up for her refusal.

Psi held her hand in his (marveling at how it fit) and listened as Cocky filled him in on how she had lost Isabel, how she had looked for the dog all day, and how she had just heard that a bomb in Isabel's collar was set to explode at four o'clock that morning and kill the Secretary of State.

"Where's your mother?" Psi asked.

Cocky shrugged. "Who knows? She went to her self-awareness class. That always takes all night."

"Well, we'll leave her a note. First we should call the Stinsons—"

"And the police," interrupted Cocky.

"Yes. We'll split up. I'll telephone the police right now, while you run over to the Stinsons' and wake them up. I'll meet you—where?"

"Back here?"

"No. On the Stinsons' corner. Look, we know where Isabel was lost. Down by Bank Street. So we begin the hunt there."

"She'd probably be trying to go home."

"Exactly. So tell the Secret Service about the bomb. Tell them to defuse it."

Cocky left a note for her mother in the front hall. It said: "Psi and I are looking for Isabel. She's been bombed."

At the Stinsons' she raced up the dark steps to the door. She could hear the jangle of the doorbell deep inside the house. There was no answer. She rang again.

"Who is it?" asked a voice over the intercom.

"It's me. Cocky Norton. I need to talk to someone right away. To Mr. Stinson."

There was silence.

Out of the corner of her eye she saw a shadow move. She whirled. A man was padding silently toward her, half hidden in the bushes.

"Don't move," he said quietly. He turned her around, patted her sides and hips. "Any weapons?"

"On me?"

He propelled her down the steps.

"But I have to talk to Mr. Stinson," she said.

"I heard you." He pushed her ahead of him, one hand on her shoulder, to the back alley, where he stopped her under the streetlight. A second agent stepped into the light.

"It's pretty late to be out ringing doorbells," said the first one angrily, dropping his pistol into a shoulder holster. He looked enormous.

"Do you know whose house this is?"

She looked desperately from one to the other. "Listen, I'm the dogwalker for the Stinsons. I walk Isabel, their basset hound." She searched their faces anxiously. "And it's a matter of life and death. Please listen to me."

"I know you," said the first agent. He stroked his full moustache. "You used to hang around the Kissingers' when he was Secretary of State. What, you got a *thing* for Secretaries of State?" He turned to his partner. "You should have seen her. She soaped the camera one day. Another day, she's out teasing Tyler, the dog." He turned on her accusingly. "Coo-coo. Or Cookie."

She blinked, not understanding.

"Or Keekoo. What's your name?"

"Cocky. I—"

"So now you're out ringing the Stinson doorbell at midnight."

"I oughta turn you over my knee."

"Please," she begged, and in her despair she brought both hands together in a gesture of prayer. "*Please*, it's a matter of life and death. This afternoon I lost Isabel, the dog."

"That's right."

She looked gratefully at the younger man. "And we've been looking all day for her," she continued. "Has she come back?"

He shook his head.

"Well, I've just discovered what's happened, and it's so awful, it's unbelievable—" The words caught in her throat.

"I don't trust this kid one minute," murmured the tall, moustached agent.

"Please, listen. I've been calling and looking for Isabel all afternoon and all this evening, and finally it got to be around ten o'clock and I was so tired I crawled under some bushes and I fell asleep. It was just a while ago. Don't look at me like that. I'm not lying. I woke up and two men were talking right next to me. And they were saying that they'd stolen Isabel when I tied her up outside the market, and they were terrorists, and one of them planted a bomb in her collar, and then they were going to bring her back and when she was home the bomb would go off and kill the Secretary of State. It's set for four o'clock this morning, and then the Secretary of State will blow up!"

The two men stared at her.

"Only what's happened is that *they've* lost Isabel too." Even to her own ears the story sounded implausible.

"So now they're looking for Isabel to get her home before the bomb goes off," she finished lamely.

There was a moment of silence, then both agents burst out laughing. They leaned against the fence and howled. They rocked back and forth. And no sooner did one begin to ease off, his laughter dying out in short gasps, than he would catch his partner's eye and begin again.

Cocky stared at them appalled. She had never imagined they would laugh. She felt the blood rush to her cheeks. Her hands trembled. Never in her wildest dreams had she thought what she would do if they didn't believe her.

"Stop it!" She stamped her foot. "Stop it! I'm not making this up."

"Sure you aren't," gasped the first agent. "Oh, jeez, I can't believe it—" And he was off again, laughing so hard he sank to the ground, his back against the fence.

"Don't worry, Cookie," the other agent said. "We'll take care of things." He ruffled her hair fondly with one hand.

"But it's true," she whispered.

"If you say so."

"You were dreaming, honey," said the younger agent. "Don't you know that? You fell asleep and had this fantastic dream. Now run on home and go to bed. It's way past your bedtime."

The moustached agent rose to his feet. He had stopped laughing, and he took two steps toward Cocky, his face dark. She froze.

"Go on!" he shouted. "Get out of here!"

For an instant Cocky thought he was going to hit her, and she flinched.

"Hey now, Joe," the younger agent soothed him.

"Listen," Cocky said, still speaking in a whisper, "if Isabel comes home tonight, please take off her collar. The bomb is in her collar. It—"

"Yeah, yeah."

She looked up at him helplessly. She searched her memory for some clue to prove the truth.

"Go on! Get out, I said. And don't you let me catch you around here again, do you hear? I've got my eye on you!"

"Yes, I'm going." She turned to the younger man, pleading. "His name was Sameer," she said. "And the other man was called Karl."

"If you don't get outta here, kid, I'm gonna take you into custody."

With a helpless look she turned and raced down the alley into the street, running, running. Her steps pounded loudly in the dark, empty street.

At the corner she slowed to a walk.

"Cocky?" Psi stepped out of the shadows.

"Oh, Psi, they didn't believe me."

124

"What happened?"

"They wouldn't listen. They thought I'd made the whole thing up. I told them to take off her collar if Isabel comes home, but I don't think they will. What about you?" she asked.

He shrugged. "My reputation preceded me as well."

"What do you mean?" She never understood him when he began to talk like that.

The police, it turned out, had first thought that he was a crank. They had ordered him off the line, then when he insisted on telling the story, they had asked his name, age, address, and school with such suspicion that he had flung down the phone.

"Oh, Psi."

"I was afraid." He hung his head.

"Of what? That I wasn't telling you the truth?"

He smiled. "No. I know that. I was afraid that when the bomb goes off and someone's hurt—"

"What?"

"—and maybe it's the Secretary of State, that they'll remember the call and think we did it." His voice sank to a whisper.

Cocky stopped dead in her tracks. "Oh, Psi."

They looked at each other for a long, horrible moment.

"They couldn't do that, could they?"

"They knew who I was," he said unhappily. "When I gave my name, the cop said, 'Aren't you the kid that started the riot on Wisconsin Avenue a few weeks ago?' "

"Oh."

"And then he'd heard a report on me this afternoon."

"But that doesn't make you—"

"Come on." Psi put one arm around her shoulder. "We don't have time to think of that. We've got about three hours left to find Isabel."

"Psi," Cocky whispered, "it's so spooky." They were in an area where the gaudy brilliant shops gave way to warehouses and abandoned factories. This section was riddled with alleys and byways, narrow twisting footpaths, and muddy walks. In the middle of the night it was ominously still.

Cocky moved closer to Psi. Their shoulders brushed.

"What's spooky is the idea of meeting those two men, looking for her too."

"Oh, wow."

They groped out of the alley toward the streetlight.

"Phototropism," Psi muttered.

"What?"

"Love of light." He laughed. "I was thinking how much braver I feel in the light."

"I know." Cocky looked at him gratefully: It was wonderful how he understood her feelings.

"Now, Cocky, we have to have a system. Look, the car with Isabel in it comes from Virginia, right? Crosses Key Bridge, and proceeds down M Street. At a certain spot it's caught in traffic. Isabel jumps out."

"We must have a hundred square blocks to hunt."

"Yes. But we know she'll probably be moving east and north, toward home. So we begin together at one corner and go around each block. You take two sides. I take two sides. We meet at the next corner. That way we cover twice as much ground."

"We split up?"

"We have to. But meet on every block."

"Okay."

"We should start here and work up toward the Stinsons." He squeezed her hand. "We may as well begin."

Cocky threw her arms around him. "I'm so glad you're here—"

Then she broke away and started down the block. "Here, Isabel," she called.

Chapter 19

Isabel shrank beneath the parked car. Four times she had tried to cross the street and each time she had been scared back by the blaring horns and rushing wheels. Around her rose a cacophony of noise and lights. Flashing red and blue strobes pierced the blackness. Raucous laughter, singing, and the high notes of band music filled the night.

It was late. It seemed hours since she had jumped from the car, and Isabel was both hungry and thirsty. Her paws hurt. Her neck itched where something under her collar irritated her skin. Her whole body ached. But mostly she was confused. She had never been out alone at night before.

She lifted her nose and sniffed. Her instinct was pulling, tugging at her to cross the street. She wanted to be moving north and east—north, across the street, and east, toward home.

She squeezed over to the sidewalk. She did not dare to cross. Her only hope lay in going around the road. She padded along the sidewalk, head low, tail dragging with exhaustion. She felt hands on her back and skittered suddenly forward, shy of being caught again.

"Oh, look at the dog."

"Here, boy. Here, boy."

But Isabel had been handled enough in one day. She shrank away and with a backward glance ran quickly off.

"Hey, looka da dog."

Now her way was barred by seven boys, arms linked. She tried to pass. Hands clutched her back, her neck, her collar. With a yelp she pulled away.

HeeeEEEAAAA! The scream came from behind, followed by the crash of a beer bottle against the brick wall and a thousand splinters of brown glass shattering at her head. The boy had thrown a bottle. She flattened against the sidewalk in terror, then dodged around the corner and down an alley, running hard. Her belly was low to the ground, stretched out. From her throat came a low whine of fear. A shooting pain stabbed her paw, and she could feel blood oozing from the cut, but she ran to the end of the alley before she slowed and stopped. She looked behind to see if the boys were following, but all was still. The alley was empty. The dark garages and warehouses around her were closed for the night. A canal ran alongside the alley. She could smell the water, and suddenly she was choked by thirst. She had had nothing to eat or drink since she had been stolen eight hours before.

She whimpered. The water lay thirty feet below her, running between high stone walls. It smelled stale and heavy with algae and slime, but Isabel had to quench her thirst.

Limping, she followed the wall until her way was blocked by a building. Then she dropped to the cobblestones and licked her hurt paw. A jagged sliver of glass was embedded in the pad. Quietly she set to work, licking, licking at the glass to get it out. When that didn't work, she tried to pull the splinter with her teeth.

Her tongue was cut and bleeding, but the splinter was still embedded in her foot.

Now the moon came up. She worked at her foot and sniffed the scent of water far below. After a time she rose and limped along the face of the building, turned down an even smaller alleyway, and traced her path eastward toward the moon.

From the main street over to her left came the shouts of

the bawdy crowd. Far to her right and far below rippled the slow waters of the canal.

Around her rose the smells of night, rich and sweet with flowering plants. The smell of spilled warm beer. Nearby a drunk was sprawled in a doorway, asleep.

Warily Isabel approached. He was dressed in filthy rags and even in his sleep he clutched to his chest a brown paper bag with a bottle of cheap wine. But it was not the wine that drew Isabel. It was the gritty end of a hot dog that had dropped to the ground beside the drunk's left shoe. Cautiously she crept forward. Her nose twitched like a living thing, independent of herself. Softly she whined, stopped, retreated a step in fear of yet another stranger, then, almost against her will, she was pulled forward by the odor of that scrap of meat. She crept up on her belly. The man was snoring. She leaped forward, grabbed it in her teeth, and in a flash was gone, bolting the frank. She licked her chops as she limped painfully on up the alley.

East. Always east. Her internal senses pointed her to the north, but always her way was blocked by buildings or by the crowds and traffic along M Street. She could not cross.

Again she lay down to rest. Again she worked at the splinter of glass in her foot, licking, biting at the glass.

The moon rose above the roofs of the houses.

From nearby she heard the slam of a screen door and a woman's voice. "Here, kitty, kittikitti. Here, kittikittikitti."

Isabel pricked her ears. She liked cats. Slowly she pulled herself to her feet. She was stiff. She moved painfully toward the sound.

The woman was outlined against the light. She wore a long thin wrapper and at her feet was a dish of—

Isabel almost fainted with delight: Chicken livers and milk!

"Why, look at you. Hello, basset."

Isabel crawled forward on her belly, nose extended. Her mournful eyes peered up at the woman.

"Come on. Who are you?" Her voice was low and sweet, and Isabel gave a friendly whine.

"Blood on your paws. Come here," she coaxed. "Come here."

She put out her hand. Isabel caught a whiff of bread and cheese, chicken livers, milk, perfume, and cat.

"Come on." How soothing was her voice! "Come on, I won't hurt you. There." She hooked her fingers in Isabel's collar. Isabel pulled back in dismay, but the woman followed, holding the collar with one hand. "There, there. You want some food?" With her free hand she reached behind her for the cat's dish, and Isabel was flooded by rich smells.

Forgotten was the hand on her collar, her cut tongue, her bleeding paw. Her nose held her glued to the dish, and the next minute her tongue was lapping up the delicious cool milk, her mouth was filled with sweetness, her stomach swelled, and Isabel nearly swooned with happiness.

Chapter 20

Karl and Sameer stopped in the shadow of an overhanging tree.

"We'll never find it," said Sameer. "Look how late it is. The moon's overhead." His knuckles cracked loudly.

Karl lit a cigar. For a moment his pudgy face was lit in the flare of the match.

Sameer took off one shoe and rubbed his sore foot.

"All right," said Karl. "Go find a pay phone. Call the police. Tell them that the Liberation Front Revolutionary Party has planted a bomb and it will go off tonight at four o'clock. Tell them it signifies our devotion to the international Cause of Freedom. We shall not submit to U.S. demands for settlement! We shall fight for the Palestinian Homeland! Never mind," he added. "I'll do it myself."

"Why don't we just tell them it's an Israeli bomb?" asked Sameer. "Then they'll get the blame."

"You mean the *credit*. Do you think we're ashamed of our cause? When we finish, the Israelis will wish they'd thought of it first."

Sameer looked up at the moon. "The bomb will go off in less than two hours."

"Come on. Let's find a phone."

Cocky and Psi walked sadly down the street. The crowds were thinning out now. A shopkeeper closed the iron gate over his display window with a squeal of hinges.

"Here, Isabel," called Cocky, but she was so tired and dejected that her voice only carried a few feet.

"It's hopeless," Psi murmured. "We aren't going to find her in time. It's three o'clock now. We have less than one hour left."

Weeeoooooooooo, whistled Cocky. "Here, Isabel."

A woman, sauntering ahead, turned at the whistle. She was dressed in black leather shorts, a gauzy white blouse, and black boots that reached above the knees. She was strolling aimlessly as if she really had no place to go.

"Here, Isabel." Cocky glanced at the woman as she passed.

The woman looked at Psi. "Looking for someone?" Her voice was low.

"A dog," Cocky answered, and stared at the woman's face, taking in with open curiosity the heavy makeup on the eyes and mouth. "We've lost our dog."

"Is it a basset hound?" asked the woman. "I—"

"Yes!"

"I found one down by the canal an hour ago. It came up as I was feeding my cat."

"Is she a female? Red and black and white?" Psi broke in. "Was she dragging a blue leash?"

"Well, you're right about the color," the woman laughed. "But she didn't have a leash. She had on a plain leather collar. And I can't swear to the sex."

"It must be her."

"I took a big chunk of glass out of her foot, but then she pulled away and ran off. She seemed like a sweet dog." She smiled again at Psi.

"Where was it?" For some reason Cocky was annoyed.

"Go down that street there and along the houses by the canal. I live at Number 321. She was just there."

"Thanks." Cocky waved a hand.

"Thank you," Psi called.

"Did you see how that woman was dressed?" Cocky asked as they trotted along.

132

Psi gave a laugh. "What do you mean?"

"She was dressed so odd. She hardly had any clothes on."

Psi pulled to a stop, laughing hard. "You're really something," he said.

"Well, I mean— Why are you laughing?" she asked. "Didn't you think it was strange?"

Psi laughed all the harder, then sobered. "Come on." He grabbed her hand. "We only have one hour to find Isabel."

When Isabel pulled free of the woman, she leaped out of reach. It was not that she didn't like the woman, but she didn't want to be caught again. She wanted to go home.

"Here, dog," the woman called after her, but Isabel broke into a fast trot, tail tight between her legs, ears flopping against her paws. She followed the street going east. She felt better with food in her belly.

To her right flowed the sluggish canal. From her left came the tug that indicated home. Surely she could find her way now.

Suddenly a cat scuttered across her path—a flash of gray in the gray night; and years of breeding took their toll. With a joyful bark Isabel exploded in wild pursuit. Her tail waved like a flag. Her baying filled the alley.

The cat leaped through the doorway of an abandoned warehouse and up the concrete steps; and hot on her tail came Isabel. Her barking hit against the concrete walls and echoed sharply in her ears, and for that moment she forgot everything in the joy of the chase. The blood of generations of rabbit-hunting hounds ran in her veins, and Isabel could no more control her instinct to pursue that flash of furry gray than a duck can forget to swim.

Over a barrel, around a pile of crates, the cat flew across the warehouse floor. Isabel swerved after it, braked with both front paws, and smashed into the crates, which collapsed behind her with a thunderous roar. Neither Isabel nor the cat paid any heed. The cat dashed on, its fur flaring like a wire brush, and right at its heels yelped Isabel. The cat was cornered. It turned, saw its path was blocked, and then leaped straight up nearly eight feet in the air, reaching for the window sill. It caught at the sill with both front paws, twisted, hung there swaying, clawing for a grip with its hind legs against the smooth cement wall. Then a toe found a crack in the wall. And with one surge the cat was on the window ledge. It stood safe, hair bristling and spitting down at Isabel, who yelped and jumped against the wall.

Then the cat shook itself, settled its fur in place, and, dainty as a queen, slipped disdainfully through the window and out into the night.

Isabel was alone. For another few minutes she continued to bark and leap proudly at the wall where the cat had been. When the cat did not reappear, she sniffed up the heady odors of the frightened tom. Then she sat down panting, her tongue lolling from her mouth. She was so pleased with herself she was ready to pop! She'd shown that cat! As soon as she sat down, however, Isabel realized how tired she was. She lay quietly and once again began to lick her sore, cracked paw.

A few minutes later she remembered home. She lifted her head and whined faintly. Again she felt the tug to the north and east. She rose and trotted around the warehouse floor, nose to the cold cement. Her toenails scratched lightly against the cement, like the skittering of rats.

At the stairwell she stopped in surprise. The door was blocked by crates. She did not remember boxes here. She tried to walk around them, but they blocked the stairwell entirely. She rose on her hind legs, testing to see if she could climb or jump across them. But the boxes shifted dangerously under her weight. She dropped to the floor and whined again, pawing at crates. She was trapped.

In another half-hour the bomb would explode.

Chapter 21

When the terrorists telephoned the police, things spun completely out of control. That happens with a war. One bad action creates others even worse, and all men suffer.

Karl made the call. He dialed the central emergency number, 911, and within seconds was connected to the Police Command.

"I wish to report," he said in his heavily accented English, "that at four o'clock this morning a bomb will go off. This bomb has been set by the Liberation Front Revolutionary Party to protest U.S. involvement in Palestine. We accept no peace settlement!"

"What?" came a voice.

But he had hung up.

To his astonishment Karl found his hands were shaking. He clenched his fist in annoyance at himself. He expected such weakness in Sameer, not in someone like himself.

"Do you think they understood?" asked Sameer with a crack of his knuckles. "Maybe we should call again."

Karl would not have been so irritated if the same idea hadn't occurred to him. He thought if he had to stay another moment with Sameer he would strangle the man.

"Let's go," he said, controlling himself. "It's time to leave. You go back to the Safe House." He meant the Virginia house where the bomb had been placed in Isabel's collar. "I'll meet you there later."

"Where are you going?"

"I have one more thing to do. You go home. Go to sleep."

He pushed Sameer toward the car and with a wave of relief saw him drive away.

As he strode quickly toward the main street, he checked his pocket for his passport. If he were lucky, he thought, he could find a cab to the airport. He wanted to leave the country at once. He had an idea things were going to get much worse.

When the police got the notice of a bomb, the report passed first slowly, then swiftly up the chain of command. The patrolman who took the call was sure it was a joke. It took him a long time to get over his surprise, and then he read and reread his scribbled notes a couple of times. Twice he listened to the call as taped. Finally, to cover his back, he telephoned his sergeant. This man, however, had heard Psi's phone call of several hours before. Without hesitation, he telephoned his captain.

The captain knew better than to make an important decision by himself. For a full five minutes he conferred with his fellow officers, before daring to wake up the Inspector, asleep in bed.

The Inspector instantly telephoned the sleeping Chief of Police.

The Chief of Police telephoned the FBI.

The FBI telephoned the Secret Service.

The Secret Service telephoned the FBI and the Washington police. Each then telephoned the Mayor, who telephoned the two local newspapers. The newspapers telephoned everyone.

The police telephoned the White House and the Secret Service. The Secret Service telephoned the Pentagon.

Meanwhile, several miles away a CIA undercover agent was listening in on the FBI lines. He passed the bomb report to the CIA night duty officer, who was drowsily watching a spy thriller on the Late Late Show. The duty officer telephoned the head of the CIA.

By now the switchboard at the White House was going crazy.

In the streets a dozen police car sirens began to wail.

The Pentagon ordered a flock of helicopters into the air.

The President prepared for evacuation from the White House.

The Secretary of State, awakened from a sound sleep, was whisked hurriedly to his wife's mother's house in Maryland.

On hearing about the bomb, two security agents posted in the Stinson garden met each other's eyes, and looked uncomfortably away. Neither said a word about the young girl who had come knocking earlier at the door.

Meanwhile, in a basement room of the Israeli Embassy several miles away, another undercover agent listened through heavy earphones to the singing telephone lines of the American government; for it is a known fact that every foreign country wiretaps and bugs the host bureaucracy, searching out its secrets.

Within minutes the Israeli Ambassador had phoned his counterpart at the Arab League.

"If you think you can get away with this, Ahmed, you're crazy," he shouted angrily in Arabic. "I know you're behind this bomb. We won't allow it!" He slammed down the phone on the Arab's shouts of protest, then picked it up again to order his men on a commando raid.

"Ahmed says they know nothing about the bomb," he told an aide, speaking in his own language. "They pretend it's an extremist group they don't control. Get over to that Safe House in Virginia and take it. I want all records. Capture everything—people too. I don't trust the Americans for one minute. With all their devotion to due process, the Americans will let the terrorists get clean away."

Through the dark night sped the Israeli commandos, across Key Bridge and out to the Virginia suburbs, toward the plain stone house where in the kitchen Sameer sat alone under the white glare of the fluorescent lights, playing solitaire. On the table at his elbow was a cup of strong tea, sweetened with milk and honey. He had been told by Karl to go to sleep; but how could he sleep when his nerves were all on edge? He was listening to the radio for news of the bomb. It was a classical-music station, playing Brahms.

Police cars wailed through the streets of Washington.

Helicopters roared high overhead.

The President was airlifted to his emergency headquarters on a mountaintop in Virginia.

The Secretary of State was pacing his mother-in-law's living room, explaining to his wife that nothing was the matter.

At 3:45 A.M. the Israeli commandos hit Sameer's house in five cars, machine guns blazing. The windows shattered. The lights went out. Sameer threw himself to the floor, hands over his head. One bullet smashed the radio, which screamed with a single piercing note of solid static.

Then ten commandos burst through the door . . .

Meanwhile the head of the Arab League had called out his bodyguard. His men, while bugging the Israeli Embassy, had overheard news of a commando attack. Ahmed was certain the target was himself. He telephoned the U.S. State Department to protest the Israeli attack. He threatened war. He telephoned the United Nations in New York to demand a peace-keeping mission. He telephoned the White House for an apology. He telephoned Beirut.

His bodyguard barricaded the doors. Hidden machine guns lifted into place, aimed on the road and walkways. They were mounted in special brackets that appeared to outsiders as ordinary flowerpots. Then, set for the siege, the Arabs waited for the attack. The first car that turned down their drive would be automatically incinerated by a firebomb. How were they to guess it would be the milkman's truck?

Chapter 22

Cocky and Psi sank to the sidewalk, their backs to the warehouse wall.

"We're too late." Psi looked at his watch. "It's three thirty."

"Well, we tried," Cocky said, numb with exhaustion.

The moon hung low in the west now, barely visible over the rooftops. A cool wind blew in from the river nearby. In the distance they could hear the steady drone of a helicopter.

"The police are looking for someone," Psi commented. "You hear the helicopter?"

"Hmm."

"They have searchlights to look into all the gardens."

"I wish they'd done it five hours ago and looked for Isabel."

They laughed, but neither thought it very funny. Now time took on a surreal and floating quality, as if for them, in their helplessness, action was suspended. They could only sit and wait; and now the night began to take its own effect, for darkness is a time of secrets shared. They sat very still, listening to the rising-falling helicopter roar. After a moment Cocky said:

"Psi, what do you want to be when you grow up?"

"Seriously?"

"Seriously."

"I don't know." He thought for a moment, then began.

"I've never told it to anyone before, but I want to do something fabulous. I want to be famous."

"Like your father."

He glanced over at her. "My father's not famous."

"You told me he was a famous phys—phy—"

"Physicist," Psi finished for her. In the darkness Cocky could not see his face. "Listen, my father's nothing. My father walked out on my mother and me when I was just born. I never even saw him till a couple years ago. Then when I was four or five, my mother left. No one wanted me."

"Oh, Psi."

"My father's a bum. He comes over every now and again. Drifts into town. I don't know how he found me. Just one day he come over once to the house," he continued. He did not know he was falling into the speech patterns of his father as he talked about him. "First time he'd ever seen me. You'd a thought he'd be proud of me. I get good marks in school. You know what he did?" He laughed bitterly. "Took a belt and beat me up."

"Oh, Psi."

"It happens ever'time. Last time I saw him was about a year later. He'd found out where I lived, see, so he come round to ask for money. He sat there, feet on the coffee table that Aunt Brenda cares about. She polishes it every Sunday. His feet up on the table. A bottle of liquor in one hand. And he called me over to him. He says, 'Come over here, you wanta Indian-wrestle?' And he teases me about my looks."

Cocky hugged her knees in the darkness and said nothing.

"So then suddenly he grabs me by the arm, twists it around. He's got a hammerlock on my arm, and he puts one knee in my back, and he says, 'Okay, now you're gonna show where Brenda keeps her money.' I couldn't move. I'm in agony. He's about to break my arm."

"What did you do?"

"I said okay. I told him, 'Let go, and sure I'll show you

where she keeps it.' So he loosens up on my arm a little but not much. He's still holding it, and I tell him it's in the sugar bowl in the kitchen, thinking he'll go look in there and I can run away."

"And did he?"

"No," Psi whispered. "He pushed me along in front of him, and I can't move practically with my arm up my back so high I'm touching my own neck, and when he got there he saw I'd lied and there wasn't any money—"

"What did he do?"

Psi laughed. "Darned if he didn't break my arm," he said. "I can't believe it. He just beat the hell out of me."

"Oh, Psi."

"I didn't tell him where the money was, neither. I run out of the house finally and got myself over to Georgetown Hospital, and then you know what?"

"What?"

He laughed again. "They wouldn't let me in without my parents' signature, 'cause I wouldn't be able to pay for treatment. I wasn't about to telephone home with that man sitting there."

"So what did you do?"

"Stayed in the waiting room for the whole night. I didn't tell them my arm was broke. Finally I got through to Aunt Brenda and the old lady come along."

"Don't talk like that," Cocky said primly. "I hate it when you talk like trash."

"Well, that's what I am, right? Next time I see him, I'm gonna knock his teeth in. I was just a little kid, then. I couldn't protect myself, but now I'm big. I've been working out."

Cocky said nothing.

"You're lucky. Your father don't hassle you."

"My father's not home," Cocky said slowly. She was thinking things out, framing words in her mind that she had never allowed herself to say before. "My father and mother got separated, and he lives in California now. He's been gone almost a year. He has a girl friend out there. He sends me a present for my birthday and Christmas."

"Well, that's nice."

"The things he sends are always too young. Like last time, he sent me a stuffed animal."

"Well, but he tried," Psi said. "Did you like it?"

"What? The stuffed animal?" He nodded, at which she ducked her head. "Actually I love it. I always go to bed with it."

"Yeah. Well, see?"

They were silent for a moment.

"Anyway, your mother's nice."

"She's okay," Cocky said. She didn't want to boast or sound too enthusiastic.

"Now me, I grew up being passed from home to home. Aunt Brenda's a relative and I've been with her longer'n anybody. But she's paid to keep me. She only does it for the money."

"Maybe she takes money," Cocky defended her. "But if she didn't love you, she'd kick you out. She really loves you a lot."

"Do you think so?" Psi's voice lifted.

"I know so."

She curled up on the ground, her head in Psi's lap. From here she could see the fading moon. "Should we be calling Isabel?"

"It's hopeless," he answered. "She's probably home at the Stinsons' by now. Getting ready to blow up the Secretary of State."

On the other side of the warehouse wall, Isabel jerked in her sleep. Her neck hurt where the lump in her collar was rubbing against her skin. She dreamed she was hunting small furry creatures through high grass, and her legs twitched.

"Quarter to four," said Psi.

"The bomb goes off in fifteen minutes," Cocky said. The

helicopters were coming closer now. There were two of them, and as they circled, their motors, coming nearer or moving away, droned steadily up and down the scale.

"I think about my mother sometimes, though," said Psi. "I mean, even though I like Aunt Brenda and all, I wonder if my mother is looking for me somewhere in the world."

"Wandering about," laughed Cocky, sitting up. "Calling for you. Calling. Because she lost you by accident."

They burst out laughing, the strain of the previous hours erupting in giddy silliness.

"And she loves me, loves me." Psi threw his arms around Cocky. "Her long lost son."

"You could wander through the world, looking for her," continued Cocky. "Like King Richard's minstrel."

"Like what?"

"Don't you know that story?" She pulled away, pleased that she knew something he did not. "We learned it in school this year. Oh, it's just beautiful. There's this King of England, and he really was a real person. His name was Richard the Lion-Hearted, because he was so brave; and one day he was captured by the enemy in a war, and he was locked up in a castle, and no one knew where he was. Or even what *country* he was in. But his faithful minstrel, who was his servant and friend, this guy found him. And guess how he did it!"

"How?"

"Well, he walked all over Europe, from one castle to the next, singing a special song under the windows of all the castles, and then one day King Richard heard him. The King was in a dungeon." She squirmed to her knees in her excitement, looking up at Psi. "And from deep underground he heard the song, and he began to sing it too, and then the minstrel knew it was Richard, and then he was ransomed and came back to England. I love that story," she finished happily.

"That's what we should've done with Isabel," Psi laughed. "Sing for Isabel."

"Like the day she won us the movie tickets."

OOOORRRrrrrrooooooooooo, he howled. They burst out laughing.

"No, no." Cocky rose to her feet. She was so tired now she was almost dizzy. "It was *On top of Ooooooooolllllldd Smoooooooooo-keeeeeeeeeee.*"

Psi joined in. "*All covered with snooooooooooooooo-wwwwww.*"

In the warehouse Isabel jerked awake.

"*I lost my truuuuuuuuuuuue loooooovv-errrrrrrrrr.*"

Their voices climbed the scale, and suddenly they were joined by a howl, a wail from behind the warehouse wall.

They froze. Isabel's howl descended to a series of frantic barks.

"*Isabel!*" shouted Cocky.

"*Hooowwwwwl!*" Psi brayed, and again Isabel joined in.

"It's her! It's her!"

"Isabel!"

"She's in this building!"

Together they scrambled around the corner, shouting at the top of their lungs. Their calls were echoed inside the building by Isabel's frantic barks.

"The door! Where's the door?"

Overhead the helicopters almost drowned them out with their roar. The searchlights swept the blackness.

"Isabel! *Wow-wow!*" Cocky called, then turned to Psi. "The time!" she screamed. "What time is it?"

"Come on!"

Psi vaulted in the door and up the circular cement stairwell. It was black as pitch, and at the top he stumbled against the boxes.

Cocky was at his heels.

"She's trapped. Hurry." Psi was throwing the boxes aside, pawing a path through the crates toward the dog. On the far side, Isabel leaped and barked with delight.

And suddenly the path was clear and with a joyous yelp Isabel threw herself at them. Her weight knocked Cocky off her feet.

144

"Isabel!"

A wet tongue was slapping her mouth and cheeks. A tail whipped across her eyes. Cocky's hands hugged the hard muscular back.

"Cocky," Psi yelled. "Get her outside. The collar! We can't see." His hands closed on the dog, pulling her toward the black steps.

"I can't see."

"Hurry." He dashed down the steps, one hand linked to the dog's collar, and once in the alley he dropped to his heels beside Isabel.

A helicopter swooped overhead, the searchlight lancing the night. It paused within a half a block of them, hung suspended.

"Wave to them!" shouted Psi above the noise. "Get their attention!"

But Cocky was kneeling beside Isabel, her fingers groping for the buckle of the collar. It was off!

"There!"

An instant later Psi snatched it from her hand. "Hold Isabel!" Then he was running, the collar held high above his head, running down the hill toward the river.

"Psi!" Cocky screamed. Her arms hugged Isabel. The searchlight splashed a yellow pool across Cocky and the dog and swept on over the rooftops, lit up Psi racing down the hill. She could see his white shirt.

"Psi!" she screamed again, as he was plunged in darkness.

The helicopter turned in a narrow circle, the searchlight piercing the streets, hunting for the running figure. It picked him up again just as he came to Water Street. A moment later he reappeared on the riverbank. For an instant he was spotlighted in the yellow beam. He slung one arm back to throw the collar into the water.

"Psi!"

The explosion seemed to rip the universe apart. An orange fireball roared above the river, consuming the highway,

145

the trees, the warehouses. The light burned her eyeballs, and the force of the explosion tossed the helicopter across the sky, its searchlight twisting crazily into the lopsided night air.

Cocky threw herself down on Isabel. *Ba-rooom! Baaa-rrooom!* She felt the earth shudder with the shock, and her world was encompassed in the howls of Isabel, the roar of flames, and the sob that tore her chest. She was awash in noise and orange flame.

Chapter 23

Cocky sat on the edge of the hospital bed. "How are you today?"

Psi was wrapped in bandages. One leg in a cast hung from a frame above the bed. His arm, also in a cast, lay heavily on the white sheet.

"I want to sign your casts. Can I?"

He managed a wan smile. "Sure. Only don't make me smile. Because it hurts."

She scrunched down on the bed and began to draw on his cast with a felt-tip pen. "Gee, what I wouldn't give for my Magic Marker set," she muttered. "This is a perfect drawing surface. I need colors." Flowers, scrolls, curlicues, butterflies rolled from the tip of her pen.

"Stop it, Cocky." He pulled up his arm. "That's enough. Tell me what happened. Tell about the news coverage."

She ignored his question and threw herself into a chair. "What's on TV? You're so lucky. I never get to watch all day."

"Nothing's on," he answered. "Now stop it. I want to hear what's been happening. Did they do the TV show on you?"

"It was great!" she laughed. "It's too bad you couldn't see it. But I gave you credit anyway."

He sank back on the pillow, listening happily.

"It was nighttime, see, and the TV cameras came right to

the house, to the front door, and they did an interview right there on the steps. They had a mobile truck with lights and sound gear and all, and when the cameras were set, the talent, who was Tom Cutler, asked me a lot of dumb questions."

"What'd he say first? How'd he introduce you?"

"Well, first he said a lot of stuff into the cameras with just his face on and not me. He said how my name was Katharine Anne Norton and about Isabel and the bomb and you—he called you Peter Ilyich—and how we had saved everyone! And then he pushed this big fat black microphone right up against my mouth so close I thought he was going to bash my teeth in, and he said, 'Well, Cocky, how does it feel to be a celebrity?' Which is a pretty dumb question, I think."

"So, what'd you say?"

"Oh, I was terrific!" she crowed. "I was so modest. I looked down to the ground and gave a little smile, and then I looked up innocently into the cameras— Oh, you would have loved it. And then I said, 'It was really nothing.' And the next thing I said was, 'My friend, Psi Ilyich, threw away the bomb.' And everybody clapped." She made a face.

"Let's see, what else did he ask? He asked what I wanted to be when I grew up, and whether I ever thought I'd be a heroine—that was the word he used. Yuck. And whether we'd been scared. Dumb stuff like that. Then he told about you and how you were too burned to be interviewed, and your broken arm and hip, but the doctors thought you'd be okay—"

"That's right," he said. "I'm going to be all right. The doctor said I would."

She looked at him without speaking.

He dropped his eyes. "I know. I may not walk straight again. He told me that too. And maybe I'll always have a limp. So I won't be a skateboard champion, that's all. But I'll be able to walk."

She looked away. She could not bear to meet his eyes.

"Listen, Cocky," he finished angrily. "I don't need you feeling sorry for me, do you hear? So I walk with a gimp. I'm alive, you hear me? And anyway, what do the doctors know? You just wait and see, I'll practice walking as soon as I get this cast off. I'll go throw baseballs. Listen, I've decided something. I'm going to walk *perfectly*. I'm going to be a great athlete. So don't waste any sympathy on old Psi." They exchanged a look. "Okay. But what I do need from you—" He grinned lopsidedly and cried *Ouch!* "What I need from you is a little of the old cock-and-bull sparkle, okay? So shut up and go on about the interview."

"Well, afterward the whole neighborhood gave a party, and all the grown-ups crowded around me for a while and asked a lot of questions and everything, until gradually they all started talking to each other ... Also, my father telephoned from California."

She stopped, thinking that over. "That was nice. He's getting married," she added. "He said he was really proud of me, and he's asked me to come out for the wedding."

"Are you going?"

She nodded. "In the fall. But then I'll be back for school. My mother cried."

"Oh."

"She was really upset. She locked herself in the bedroom for a while. But then the grown-ups were having this big cocktail party, and they were all drinking and shouting and laughing, so Mom came out and she was laughing harder'n anybody practically. She stayed up almost the whole night. I went up to bed. I was tired."

"Is she all right?"

"I guess so. Things are rough for her right now." She jumped up. "Hey, let me draw one more picture on your cast. There's a wonderful crack in your leg cast. It looks just like a tree. Don't look." She was silent for a few moments as she concentrated. "There." She drew back proudly from her work. "They caught the spy in Mr. Stinson's office. He confessed everything."

"I know. I heard it on the news."

"That's how they got the briefcase—with his help."

"I know."

"I think it's terrible. That's how the terrorists knew the plans and always knew where Mr. Stinson was."

"Cocky, I know!" Psi said.

"And they also caught one of the terrorists. His name is Sameer something."

"I know."

"The Israelis have him."

"Cocky, I saw it too."

"By the way, I'm to tell you that the President says he's not giving the awards until you're out of the hospital."

"The *what*?"

She burst into a wide grin. "I knew you'd just die! Isn't it terrific? We're heroes. We're each going to get a medal! And the President of the United States will present it himself in a ceremony in the Rose Garden of the White House."

"Holy geez."

"I know." She laughed. "Can you imagine? But that won't happen till you get out."

"They'd better ask the press," he muttered. "I want my turn this time."

"Only if you give the credit to me! I heard about the ceremony today from Mr. Stinson," she continued. "They're going to ask all of Congress and the diplomats, too, from the Middle East and France and England and all. Mr. Stinson said at first he was thinking of giving us a small reception at the State Department, and then they decided the President ought to do it at the White House. And it's gotten bigger and bigger. It's going to be televised over network TV."

"Holy geez."

"I think Isabel should get a medal too."

"*Ow!* Oh, you know I can't laugh!"

"And meanwhile, if you hurry up and get out, there's a really good flick at the Key theater. I can get you in for free."

Suddenly he sat up to peer at her face. "Hey, Cocky, what have you done to your eyes?"

She straightened with a vague, distant look. "Oh, nothing."

"They look all black. Have you got some kinda stuff on them?"

"I was just trying something out," she said with dignity. "It's nothing." She felt uncomfortable under his scrutiny.

"It's mascara!" He burst out laughing. "*Ouch!*" Then seeing her expression, his voice softened and he said, "Hey, well, it looks okay, you know?"

"Do you think so?"

"Yeah. But I think you're too young to wear that stuff. I hate that muck."

"Well, I have to grow up sometime. Anyway, I only put it on to practice for the TV."

"Yeah, well, I guess you're right. It looks, you know, kind of pretty."

Cocky breathed a sigh of satisfaction. For that moment her heart was filled with utter happiness.

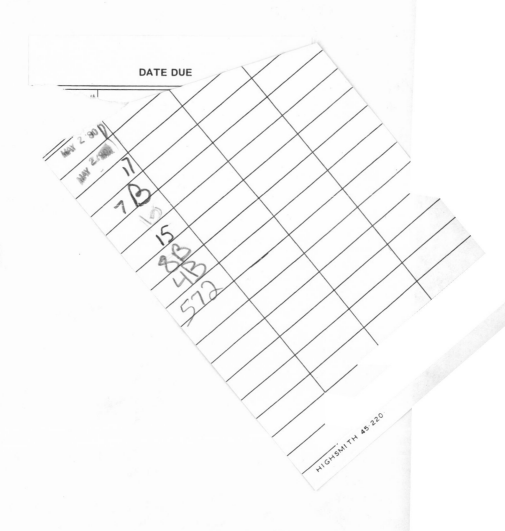

DATE DUE

MAY 2 '90

MAY 2 '90

HIGHSMITH 45-220